AF604680

THE TENCYCLOPEDIA

OTHER BOOKS BY THE AUTHOR

The Battle for BHP

The Cricket War: The Inside Story of Kerry Packer's World Series Cricket

The Border Years

One Summer, Every Summer: An Ashes Journal

Australian Cricket Anecdotes

The Summer Game: Australian Test Cricket 1949–71

One of a Kind: The Story of Bankers Trust Australia 1969–99

Mystery Spinner: The Story of Jack Iverson

The Big Ship: Warwick Armstrong and the Making of Modern Cricket

Endless Summer: 140 Years of Australian Cricket in Wisden

The Vincibles

Bad Company: The Strange Cult of the CEO

The Uncyclopedia

Game for Anything: Writings on Cricket

10. *Ten* was the first album by Pearl Jam (1991), the tenth album by LL Cool J (2002), a film by Blake Edwards (1979) and by Abbas Kiarostami (2002), is a Japanese comic, and the official periodical of the Australian Gymnastics Federation.

THE SUPERSTITIONS OF TEN GREAT MEN

1. *Hans Christian Andersen* had a fear of premature burial and slept with a note by his bedside saying: 'I only seem dead.'

2. Grand Prix driver *Alberto Ascari* was acutely fearful of black cats and would find an alternative route if one crossed his path while driving.

3. Baseballer *Wade Boggs* of the Boston Red Sox and New York Yankees had to eat chicken and cheesecake before every game, and two hot dogs and a bag of barbecue potato chips washed down with iced tea afterwards.

4. *Enrico Caruso* would never travel on Fridays, and was convinced that he could protect his health by keeping a dried anchovy suspended over his chest, hanging from a necklace.

5. *Charles Dickens* would always align his bed with the North Pole.

6. *Peter the Great* was afraid of crossing bridges.

7. *Elvis Presley* always wore a Christian cross, a Star of David, and the Hebrew letter 'chi', explaining that he did not want 'to miss out on heaven due to a technicality'.

8-10. *Franklin Roosevelt* and *Arnold Schoenberg* were both triskaidekaphobic: Roosevelt would never sit at a table of thirteen, while Schoenberg would take to his bed on the thirteenth day of every month fearful of misfortune (he died on 13 July 1951). *Woodrow Wilson*, by contrast, thought thirteen his lucky number, and en route to the Paris Peace Conference asked that the ship be slowed down so that he could reach Europe on the thirteenth of the month.

TEN

1. Ten, the natural number after nine and preceding eleven, is a composite number, the sum of the first three prime numbers (2+3+5), and of the first four digits (1+2+3+4).

2. Ten is the base of the decimal numeral system, the most common system for denoting numbers in spoken and written language. Thus, any number can be instantly multiplied by ten by adding a zero (124 x 10=1240).

3. The Greeks saw ten as auspicious: the siege of Troy lasted ten years; Odysseus returned home after ten years of wandering. Pythagoreans regarded ten as the holiest of numbers and took their oaths upon it, as it was the number of their Tetraktys 'from which eternal nature springs and in which it is rooted'.

4. The Romans made ten the basis of their numbering system. Their original calendar had ten months, six of thirty days and four of thirty-one days, totalling 304 days. It featured, in April, a ten-day festival held in honour of Ceres, goddess of agriculture, culminating in the Cerealia.

5. The Mayans regarded ten as highly inauspicious, believing that every tenth day belonged to the death god, since it followed the ninth day, which they deemed the day of disease.

6. The Bambara people of Mali consider ten very lucky, connecting its status as the sum of the first four digits to the four stages of creation, and believing it a symbol of fertility.

7. Ten features recurrently in the theologies of Christianity, Judaism, Hinduism, Buddhism, Sikhism and other religions.

8. In Afrikaans, ten is *tien*; in French, *dix*; in German, *zehn*; in Greek, *dhéka*; in Italian, *dieci*; in Portuguese, *dez*; in Russian, *désyat*; in Scots, *ten*; in Spanish, *diez*; in Swedish, *tio*; in Welsh, *deg*.

9. In binary code, 10 represents 2, relating it to the sources of the multiple, and is represented by 1010, a form of self-replication.

With thanks and best wishes to Sally Warhaft, Philippa Hawker, David Studham, Melanie Ostell, George Thomas and Cath Ertler.
Non quaeras quis hoc dixerit; sed, quis diciatur attende.

The Text Publishing Company
171 La Trobe Street
Melbourne Victoria 3000
Australia
www.textpublishing.com.au

First published 2004

Designed by Peter Long
Line drawings on pages 31, 40, 58, 110, 118–19, 145 and 149 by Bill Wood Illustrations
Typeset in ACaslon by J & M Typesetting
Printed and bound by Griffin Press

National Library of Australia
Cataloguing-in-Publication data:

Haigh, Gideon.
The Tencyclopedia.

ISBN 1 920885 35 8.

1. Curiosities and wonders - Australia. 2. Australia - Miscellanea. I. Title.

994

Gideon Haigh

Text Publishing
Melbourne Australia

TEN POKER HANDS

From highest to lowest:

Royal flush:	ace, king, queen, jack, 10 of same suit.
Straight flush:	five cards of a suit in sequence (eg 6, 7, 8, 9, 10 of spades).
Four-of-a-kind:	four cards of same rank (eg 7 of clubs, hearts, spades, diamonds).
Full house:	three of a kind (eg three queens) and a pair (eg two jacks).
Flush:	five cards of same suit.
Straight:	five cards in sequence.
Three-of-a-kind:	three cards of same rank.
Two pair:	two cards of the same rank twice.
One pair:	two cards of the same rank.
High card:	highest-ranking card in a hand.

TEN MASSES

Mass in kilograms

10^{-30}	electron
1.7×10^{-27}	proton
4×10^{-25}	uranium atom
10^{-22}	haemoglobin molecule
5×10^{-7}	grain of sand
7×10^{22}	Moon
6×10^{24}	Earth
2×10^{30}	Sun
10^{41}	Milky Way
10^{52}	observable universe

TEN REMARKS OF RONALD REAGAN

'I'd like to keep making horse operas. I'm a ham—always was, always will be.'
Retiring as president of Screen Actors Guild but disavowing interest in a political career, 1953.

'I'd like to harness their youthful energy, with a strap.'
After student demonstrations in California, 1966.

'We should declare war on North Vietnam. We could pave the whole country and put parking stripes on it and still be home by Christmas.'
Proposing foreign policy, 1966.

'A tree's a tree. How many do you need to look at?'
Responding to plans to expand California's Redwood National Forest, 1967.

'If it's a bloodbath they want, let's get it over with.'
Concerning student demonstrations, 1970.

'You can tell a lot about a fellow's character by his way of eating jellybeans.'
In the *New York Times*, 1981.

'An evil empire.'
Of the Soviet Union, 1983.

'We are especially not going to tolerate these attacks from outlaw states run by the strangest collection of misfits, Looney Tunes, and squalid criminals since the advent of the Third Reich.'
After the hijacking of an American airliner, 1985.

'Facts are stupid things.'
At the Republican National Convention, 1988, several times. Attempting to quote John Adams: 'Facts are stubborn things.'

'They say hard work never killed anyone, but I say: why take a chance?'
Attributed.

15

Anne Frank (1929–1945)
Died in concentration camp
Symbol of Jewish suffering under Nazism; author of *Diary of a Young Girl* (1947).

16

Lady Jane Grey (1537–1554)
Executed
Pretender to English throne, queen for nine days.

John Travers Cornwell (1900–1916)
Died of wounds
Boy, first class, on HMS *Chester*; won posthumous Victoria Cross at Battle of Jutland, May 1916.

17

Thomas Chatterton (1752–1770)
Suicide by poison
Self-destructive boy poet, author of 'Ballade of Charatie'.

Richie Valens (1941–1959)
Killed in plane crash
Guitarist, vocalist, born Richard Steven Valanzuela, died with Buddy Holly and the Big Bopper.

18

Tutankhamen (c. 1341–1323 B.C.)*
Boy pharaoh, twelfth king of the eighteenth dynasty, crowned at age of nine.

Jimmy King (1949–1967)
Killed in plane crash
Guitarist with the Bar Kays, backing band for Otis Redding, died with him and three other teenage band members.

19

Joan of Arc (1412–1431)
Burned as heretic
French heroine, Maid of Orleans.

Martin Lamble (1950–1969)
Killed in car crash
Original drummer in folk-rock group Fairport Convention; Richard Thompson's girlfriend Jeannie Franklyn died in same accident.

Nicholas Traina (1978–1997)
Suicide by overdose
Lead singer of Link 80, son of author Danielle Steel, suffered from bipolar disorder and heroin addiction, subject of her memoir *One Bright Light* (1998).

---

*In dispute. Originally believed to have died of natural causes; theories of murder subsequently advanced.

TEN PLAGUES OF EGYPT

1. The Nile and other Egyptian waters run with blood.
2. Frogs swarm from the Nile invading Egyptian homes.
3. Lice form from the dust of Egypt.
4. Swarming flies.
5. Pestilence annihilates Egyptian livestock.
6. Epidemic of boils from furnace soot that Moses tosses into the air.
7. Hailstorm kills plant life and crops.
8. A plague of locusts consumes the new shoots.
9. A darkness lasts three days.
10. Passover: God kills the firstborn of all Egyptians.

TEN WORKS OF ENGLISH LITERATURE THAT WE COULD DO WITHOUT

Brigid Brophy, Michael Levey and Charles Osborne begin their *Fifty Works of English Literature We Could Do Without* (1967) with a challenge: 'Before you let fly with a scream at our iconoclasm, pause and play fair: do you really like, admire and (most important criterion of all) enjoy the works in question, or do you merely think you ought to? English literature...is choked with the implied obligation to like dull books.' Here are ten, with a sample of the authors' waspish opinions:

1. *Beowulf*: 'Admiring comment on its poetry is about as relevant as praise for the architecture of Stonehenge.'
2. William Shakespeare's *Hamlet*: 'The posturing, egotistical, baby-cum-adolescent in us all.'
3. John Bunyan's *Pilgrim's Progress*: 'Like the gentlemen who walk through the West End of London with sandwich-boards imploring us to flee from the wrath to come.'
4. Charles Dickens' *Pickwick Papers*: 'This distressingly jolly charade...written in a series of jerkily spasmodic bouts of inane euphoria.'
5. Charlotte Bronte's *Jane Eyre*: 'Like gobbling a jar-full of school-girl stick-jaw.'
6. R. D. Blackmore's *Lorna Doone*: 'Devonian clotted-cream smugness.'
7. Mark Twain's *Huckleberry Finn*: 'Canned huckleberries in the unnatural juice of homely humour.'
8. D. H. Lawrence's *Lady Chatterley's Lover*: 'Under-the-hairdryer reading.'
9. Rupert Brooke's *1914 Sonnets*: 'Don't go in for flag-waving if you're limp-wristed.'
10. Edith Sitwell's *Collected Poems*: 'Verse in the style of Churchill's war speeches.'

Archimedes' Principle

'The buoyant force of a submerged object is equal to the weight of the fluid that is displaced by that object.'

One of the founding principles of hydrostatics propounded by the Greek philosopher and mathematician Archimedes (287–212 B.C.), apocryphally after a bath in his home city of Syracuse.

Bernoulli's Principle

'As the velocity of a fluid increases, its pressure decreases.'

Originally an insight in hydrodynamics by Daniel Bernoulli (1700–1782), one of a gifted family of polymaths from Antwerp, who held chairs in anatomy, botany and physics at Basle. It is now commonly invoked in aerodynamics, especially in explanation of the shape of the wings of aircraft, the tops curved and undersides flat: air travels slower on the bottom (creating more pressure) and faster on top (creating less pressure), thus keeping the plane airborne.

Dilbert Principle

'The most ineffective workers are systematically moved to the place where they can do the least damage—management.'

Conclusion of cartoonist and satirist Scott Adams (b. 1957) in the bestselling compilation of his comic strips, *The Dilbert Principle* (1996). He also promotes as a corollary a 'sophisticated theory' to explain aberrant behaviour within organisations: 'People are idiots.'

Heisenberg's Uncertainty Principle

'The position and momentum of any body or particle cannot be simultaneously determined.'

Largely for this crucial insight in quantum mechanics was the German theoretical physicist Werner Heisenberg (1901–1976) awarded a Nobel Prize in 1933. Also known as the principle of indeterminacy, it is now invoked in other sciences where there are questions of ambiguity and elasticity. Because Heisenberg thought that 'the more precisely the position is determined, the less precisely the momentum is known', it is held safer to refer to statistical probabilities than to formulate general laws.

The Lucifer Principle

'Evil is a by-product of nature's strategies for creation and is woven into our most basic biological fabric.'

Central contention of *The Lucifer Principle: A Scientific Expedition into the Forces of History* (1995) by the American social scientist and controversialist Howard Bloom (b. 1946), and part of his ongoing exploration of the 'mass mind', applying recent scientific developments to old conundrums of human behaviour. Not merely is 'evil' a naturally occurring phenomenon, but human instinct for communal behaviour manifests the existence of 'superorganisms', like those formed in nature by amoeba and sponges: 'We cannot live in total separation from the human clump.'

Mach's Principle

'The inertial effects of mass are not innate in a body, but arise from its relation to the totality of other masses.'

Proposed by Ernst Mach (1838–1916) in *The Science of Mathematics* (1893), written while he held the chair in physics at Prague. Disputing the sense of assessing acceleration of a mass relative to absolute space, he thought it more useful to speak of acceleration relative to the distant stars, inertial forces having a far greater range than gravitational forces.

Pareto Principle

'A minority of input produces the majority of results.'

This lasting and now widely applied insight of the Italian economist Vilfredo Pareto (1848–1923) emerged from a study of the pattern of wealth distribution in a number of countries revealing the common characteristic that about 80 per cent of the wealth was controlled by a consistent minority of about 20 per cent of the people. Far from deploring income inequality in his *Manuale di Economia Politica* (1906), he described it as a 'predictable imbalance'.

Parmenides' Principle

'Anything rationally conceivable must exist.'

A deduction of the pioneering Greek metaphysician and atomist Parmenides of Elea (c. 514–440 B.C.) in his only surviving work *On Nature*. Non-being is not a thing and can neither be thought of nor spoken about in any meaningful or coherent way. He forbade talking as if there are possible things that nonetheless do not exist.

Peter Principle

'Employees within an organisation will advance to their highest level of competence and then be promoted to and remain at a level at which they are incompetent.'

A popular saw of organisational life advanced by Canadian educator Laurence J. Peter (1919–1990) in *The Peter Principle* (1969), co-written with Raymond Hull. Examples ranged from Nero ('A competent fiddler who achieved his level of incompetence as an administrator') to Nixon ('Author of a successful book *Six Crises*, later unable to communicate a simple message such as "I am not a crook."').

Principle of Sufficient Irritation

'Eons ago, in the remote past, a bit of inanimate matter had become so irritated by something that it crawled away, moved by indignation.' Thus Doc Labyrinth in 'Left Shoe, My Foot' aka 'The Short Happy Life of the Brown Oxford' (1952), a short story by Philip K. Dick (1928–1982). The observation inspires him to build an irritation machine so powerful as to bring inanimate matter to life; the story ends with an animated Brown Oxford man's shoe disappearing into a hedge with an animated high-heel shoe. Rustling sounds ensue.

TEN AVATARS OF VISHNU

Fish — Tortoise — Hog — Lion — Dwarf — Ram — Purushu Ram — Krishna — Horse — Another to come (Kalki Avatara)

TEN FICTIONAL ALTERNATIVE WORLDS

THE ALTERATION — Kingsley Amis (1976)
Reformation never occurred; Catholicism remains predominant.

QUEEN VICTORIA'S BOMB — Ronald W. Clark (1967)
Atomic bomb developed by scientists in Victorian England.

SS-GB — Len Deighton (1978)
Britain surrendered to Germany in February 1941; Churchill executed, King imprisoned.

THE MAN IN THE HIGH CASTLE — Philip K. Dick (1962)
US lost World War II, west occupied by Japan, east by Germany.

THE DIFFERENCE ENGINE — William Gibson & Bruce Sterling (1990)
Charles Babbage's pioneering 'computer' precipitates technological revolution in Victorian England.

THE TRANSATLANTIC TUNNEL, HURRAH! — Harry Harrison (1972)
War of Independence never occurred; US remains part of British Empire.

BRING THE JUBILEE — Ward Moore (1953)
South won the Civil War and imposed an austere peace.

THE GATE OF WORLDS — Robert Silverberg (1967)
Western civilisation did not recover from the Black Death.

THE INDIANS WON — Martin Cruz Smith (1970)
Americans westward advance thwarted.

THE AQUILIAD — S. M. Somtow (1983)
The Americas form part of the Roman Empire. Two other novels on the same premise followed: *Aquila and the Iron Horse* and *Aquila and the Sphinx*.

TEN CRIMES FOR WHICH THE SENTENCE WAS TRANSPORTATION

Patrick Colquohon's *A Treatise on the Police of the Metropolis* (1795) enumerates a host of 'Single Felonies' punishable by transportation to Australia, or whipping, 'the Pillory and Hard Labour in Houses of Correction'. These are ten:

1. Ripping and stealing Lead, Iron, Copper & c., or buying and receiving.
2. Setting fire to Underwood.
3. Stealing Letters, or destroying a Letter or Packet, advancing the Postage and secreting the Money.
4. Stealing Fish from a Pond or River—Fishing in enclosed Ponds, and buying stolen Fish.
5. Stealing Roots, Trees or Plants, of the value of *5s* or Destroying them.
6. Stealing Children with their apparel.
7. Assaulting and Cutting or Burning Clothes.
8. Cutting or Stealing Timber Trees & c. & c.
9. Stealing a Shroud out of a Grave.
10. Watermen carrying too many passengers in the Thames, if any drowned.

TEN TRADITIONAL BEER MEASURES

1 nip = 1/4 pint
1 small = 1/2 pint
1 large = 1 pint
1 flagon = 1 quart
1 anker = 10 gallons
1 firkin = 9.8 gallons
1 barrel = 31 1/2 gallons
1 hogshead = 2 barrels
1 butt = 2 hogsheads
1 tun = 2 butts

TEN ADVERTISING SLOGANS

At the end of 1999, the US marketing industry journal *Advertising Age* polled a group of experts to adduce their views of the ten most successful advertising slogans of the twentieth century. These were the findings:

Diamonds are forever	DeBeers
Just do it	Nike
The pause that refreshes	Coca-Cola
Tastes great, less filling	MillerLite
We try harder	Avis
Good to the last	Maxwell House
Breakfast of champions	Weeties
Does she...or doesn't she?	Clairol
When it rains it pours	Morton Salt
Where's the beef?	Wendy's

AN AUSTRALIAN TEN

'I like Aeroplane jelly'	Aeroplane jelly
'Mine tinkit they fit'	Pelaco
'It's moments like these you need Minties'	Minties
'Anyhow'	Winfield cigarettes
'The health food of a nation'	Peters ice cream
'I allus has wan at eleven'	Carlton & United Breweries
'Out of the blue comes the whitest wash'	Reckitt's Blue
'Keep that schoolgirl complexion'	Palmolive
'Don't argue—Hutton's is best'	Hutton's smallgoods
'Is Don, is good'	Don smallgoods

GREAT SOUTH CENTRAL PACIFIC AND MEXICAN RAILWAY

Anthony Trollope's *The Way We Live Now* (1872)

'The grandest enterprise which has ever opened itself before a public', formed to lay a 3200km rail track from Salt Lake City to Vera Cruz, promoted by the 'vile City ruffian' Augustus Melmotte and aspiring American robber baron Hamilton Fisker. Melmotte fast makes his pile, between becoming an MP and hosting banquets for the royal family and lord mayor, but succumbs to 'a self-confidence inspired...by the worship of other men which clouded his intellect'; Fisker goes on to greener swindles.

UNIVERSAL BANK

Emile Zola's *L'Argent* (1891)

Corrupt financial conglomerate based on l'Union Generale, a French bank that collapsed in 1888. The eighteenth novel in Zola's Rougon-Macquart cycle takes up the story of money-mad Aristide Saccard, who had appeared in two earlier instalments: *La Fortune des Rougon* (1871) and *La Curée* (1874). Saccard learns from a young engineer, Hamelin, of deposits of silver and iron-ore in Palestine, and founds the Universal Bank to fund their exploitation, which encourages him to further and wilder speculations. But a counterplot by Saccard's nemesis, the Jewish plutocrat Gunderman, bursts the bubble. An updated silent adaptation was filmed in 1929 by Marcel L'Herbier with Pierre Alcover as Saccard.

DAWSON T. HUNZIKER & CO

Sinclair Lewis' *Arrowsmith* (1922)

A Pittsburgh-based drug company that falsely promises the earth to high-minded Max Gottlieb. Having been offered a pure research job that appeals to his ideals, Gottlieb learns from the company's eponymous founder that the bottom line is after all a consideration: 'Personally I should like nothing so much as to spend my whole life in just producing one priceless scientific discovery, without consideration of mere profit. But we have our duty towards the stockholders of the Dawson Hunziker Company to make money for them. Do you realise that they have—and many of them are poor widows and orphans—invested their Little All in our stock, and that we must keep faith? I am helpless; I am but their Humble Servant.'

PROBITY TRUST

F. Scott Fitzgerald's *The Great Gatsby* (1924)

Having bought 'a dozen volumes on banking and credit and investment securities' which 'stood on my shelf in red and gold like new money from the mint', Nick Carroway trades bonds at this financial institution, thus entering the circles of Jay Gatsby. Gatsby himself cavorts with the likes of Newton Orchid, 'who controlled Films Par Excellence', and 'Rot-Gut' Ferret, whose gambling losses are offset by trading gains in Associated Traction. A quote from the novel regarding Gatsby is Bill Gates' favourite: 'He had come a long way to this blue lawn, and his dream must have seemed so close that he could hardly fail to grasp it.'

PYM'S PUBLICITY

Dorothy L. Sayers' *Murder Must Advertise* (1933)

London-based advertising firm where Lord Peter Wimsey goes undercover to investigate the mysterious death of a copywriter called Dean. 'We spend our whole time asking intimate questions of perfect strangers and it naturally blunts our finer feelings,' extemporises one of Dean's colleagues, Ingleby: '"Mother! Has Your Child Learnt Regular Habits?" "Are You Troubled With Fullness after Eating?" "Are you satisfied about your Drains?" "Are you Sure that your Toilet-Paper is Germ-Free?" "Your most Intimate Friends dare not Ask you this Question." "Do you Suffer from Superfluous Hair?"...Upon my soul, I sometimes wonder why the long-suffering public doesn't rise up and slay us.' Then the bodies begin piling up and it seems almost as if they have.

TREDWAY CORPORATION

Cameron Hawley's *Executive Suite* (1952)

Based in Millburgh, Pennsylvania, the third-largest manufacturer of fine furniture in the United States, founded by its tyrannical chairman Avery Bullard. The novel's first line—'A minute or two before or after two-thirty on the afternoon on the twenty-second of June, Avery Bullard suffered what was subsequently diagnosed as a cerebral hemorrhage'—sets the scene for boardroom blood-letting. Bullard had been about to announce his successor; five candidates are left to vie: J. Walter Dudley, Don Walling, Fred Alderson, Jesse Grimm and Loren Shaw. In Robert Wise's 1954 screen adaptation, the role of Walling is played by William Holden.

TAGGART TRANSCONTINENTAL

Ayn Rand's *Atlas Shrugged* (1957)

American railroad giant where Dagny Taggart and brother James wrestle for commercial and philosophical control. Beautiful Dagny is a distaff version of TT's founder Nathaniel, 'a ragged young adventurer' who had 'never accepted the creed that others had the right to stop him'; aqueous James mouths pieties like 'it seems to me there are more important things in life than making money'. It is James, however, who is in harmony with a US in the grip of crypto-socialist statutes like the Public Stability Law, the Equalization of Opportunity Law, the Fair Share Law and the Preservation of Livelihood Law, and an intelligentsia for which 'the novel of the century' is *The Vulture Is Molting*, a 'penetrating study of a businessman's greed' and 'a fearless revelation of man's depravity'.

BOSTON AND NORTHEASTERN LIFE

Philip Roth's *Portnoy's Complaint* (1967)

Insurance company that employs Alex Portnoy's thwarted and constipated father. A framed photograph of president N. Everett Lindabury hangs in the Portnoy family's hall, Alex observes, where it is as much torment as tribute: '"Mr Lindabury", "The Home Office"...my father made it sound to me like Roosevelt in the White House in Washington...and all the while how he hated their guts, Lindabury's particularly, with his corn-silk hair and his crisp New England speech, his sons in Harvard College and the daughters in finishing school, oh the whole pack of them up in Massachusetts, *shkotzim* fox-hunting! playing polo!...and thus keeping him, you see, from being a hero in the eyes of his wife and children.'

FIRST MERCANTILE AMERICAN BANK

Arthur Hailey's *The Moneychangers* (1975)

Big American bank where size matters: 'In First Mercantile American...an acknowledged status symbol was the size of a loan which a bank official had power to sanction.' Competing to be boss lender are two executive vice-presidents: slick Roscoe Heyward and sober Alex Vandervoort, who is nonetheless compromised by his affair with lawyer Margot Bracken, to whom he has turned for solace because of his wife's mental illness. Eventful plot kept the book at the top of the *New York Times* bestseller list for fourteen weeks. Adapted for a mini-series starring Kirk Douglas and Christopher Plummer in 1976.

CLARE SOAP AND CHEMICAL COMPANY

Richard Powers' *Gain* (1998)

Consumer goods giant founded by three Boston merchants in the 1830s, which makes it big with the rise of urban gentility: 'Native Balm Soap with secret extract of Healing Root will cure several cutaneous and dermal disorders, including, but not limited to, pimples, Salt Rheum, freckling and discoloration, etc. It will remove Tetter, heal ruptures and boils, firm the muscle, and prevent many further diseases of the skin as well as graver body disorders.' Clare's story is narrated in parallel with that of a realtor, Laura Bodey, whose ovarian cyst seems related to pollution in the company town of Lacewood, Illinois.

TEN LONGEST BONES IN THE HUMAN BODY

Femur • Tibia • Fibula • Humerus • Ulna • Radius • Seventh rib • Eighth rib • Innominate bone (hip) • Sternum

THE HISTORY OF CHOPPER READ IN 10½ CHAPTERS

'I did get away with one of the biggest unsolved crimes in Australia's history. I got away with writing those books. When they've forgotten all the other nitwits, they will remember Chopper Read.' Thus Mark Brandon Read (b. 1954), sometime standover man, oftentime jailbird, whose career as a literary celebrity began in early 1991 when he was interviewed at length by *Herald Sun* investigative journalist John Silvester. Two years of disarmingly detailed correspondence followed, which formed the basis of *From the Inside* and *Hits and Memories*, edited by Silvester and Andrew Rule of the *Age*.

Chopper 1: *From the Inside: The Confessions of Mark Brandon Read* (1991)
'We had fun before he died. Played a little game called Knee Cap.'

Chopper 2: *Hits and Memories: More Confessions of Mark Brandon Read* (1992)
'He looked quite surprised when I pulled out my trusty meat cleaver and slammed it down on the bar, removing his four fingers at the knuckle.'

Chopper 3: *How to Shoot Friends and Influence People* (1993)
'Death never brawls in the street. Death never has to throw a punch. Death merely smiles, puts his hand inside his coat, and says, "Excuse me, mate. I didn't quite hear that. Were you talking to me?"'

Chopper 4: *For the Term of His Unnatural Life* (1994)
'Another bright spark took early parole. He hanged himself ten minutes before lunch. We had Chiko Rolls too. Yummy.'

Chopper 5: *Pulp-Faction: Revenge of the Rabbit Kisser and other Jailhouse Stories* (1995)
'I stepped toward Georgie, took out my Beretta and brought it down across her face. Her top lip and top teeth exploded in a shower of blood.'

Chopper 6: *No Tears for a Tough Guy* (1996)
'The Kid had heard a story once about a big roll of cash being flushed down the toilet by a speed freak who…thought the flat he was in was about to be raided any minute. It took him an hour to flush all the money, and when someone did knock…later that morning he shot himself in the head rather than be taken alive…The bloke at the door was the plumber who had come to unblock the dunny.'

Chopper 7: *The Singing Detective* (1997)
'A master of the legal twist / A shrewd and artful dodge man / The man I swear this ditty to / The one and only Hodgman.'
Of his barrister, Michael Hodgman QC.

Chopper 8: *The Sicilian Defence* (1998)
'She protested that she wasn't a good dancer and received a beating that went far beyond her sick sexual masochistic fantasies…She was supplied with a new set of high heels and a new set of high-cut knickers, and felt no pain after another taste of heroin.'

Chopper 9: *The Final Cut* (2000)
'When I was sixteen [Christopher] Flannery's reputation in Melbourne overshadowed my own for violence. When I was seventeen it didn't. You can achieve a lot in the underworld in a year if you are keen and a little crazy.'

Chopper 10½: *The Popcorn Gangster* (2001)
'I could just be pulling your leg. I am, after all, a storyteller, and this could just be another story, just one more book of mischief written by a no-eared fool. But then you must ask yourself if the no-eared fool is telling lies all the time, or just some of the time.'

Read has always maintained that his books are drawn from life, while professing an allegiance to one modern author: Helen Demidenko. A film adapted from his works appeared in 2002, and he is the basis of a character in William Gibson's *Idoru* (1996). Learning of this, Read allegedly responded: 'I knew a cyberpunk once. I pulled his teeth out with pliers.'

TEN REMARKS IN PRAISE OF THE ORGAN

What with the sound of the bellows, the noise of the cymbals and the united strain of the organ pipes, the common folk stand with wondering faces, trembling and amazed.
Ailred, Abbot of Rievaulx (1109–66)

Without peer in the making of music.
J. S. Bach (1685–1750)

An organist who is master of his instruments is a virtuoso of the highest order.
Ludwig van Beethoven (1770–1827)

Money must be raised to buy organs and to train boys to squeal.
Erasmus (1466–1536)

The Swete Orgayne comforteth stedfaste mynde.
Leckingford proverb (c. 1520)

In my eyes and ears the organ will ever be the king of instruments.
W. A. Mozart (1756–1791)

Almighty God alone can never be given sufficient thanks for having granted to man in His mercy and great goodness such gifts as have enabled him to achieve such a perfect, one might almost say the most perfect, creation and instruments of music as is the organ in its arrangement and construction.
Michael Praetorius (1571–1621)

The struggle for the good organ is to me a part of the struggle for truth.
Albert Schweitzer (1875–1965)

No instrument is capable of such noble or dignified effects as the organ, and also...offers such temptations to triflers.
William Leslie Sumner (1904–1976)

To play the organ properly one should have a vision of eternity.
Charles-Marie Vidor (1845–1937)

CAPE PLEASANT GOLF CLUB

P. G. Wodehouse's 'Archibald's Benefit' in *The Man Upstairs and Other Stories* (1913)

Sleepy New Jersey club populated by 'easygoing refugees from other and more exacting clubs…who pottered rather than raced round the links', where thirty-one-year-old Archibald Mealing is a member, despite playing a game that is a 'blend of hockey, Swedish drill, and buck-and-wing dancing'. To his delight, after assiduous practice, Mealing becomes club champion—but this brings him into conflict with the dislikeable stockbroker member Gossett.

TILLINGFOLD

Hugh de Selincourt's *The Cricket Match* (1924)

A sleepy village in the lee of the South Downs whose cricket team, led by long-suffering Paul Gauvinier, faces its annual derby against rival Raveley on 4 August 1921. A tense fight is had, with a brave last-wicket stand and a breathless finish. 'If there is a better game than cricket,' exclaims one character, 'I would like to know it!' The same characters appear in *The Game of the Season* (1932) and *The Saturday Match* (1937). Gauvinier also re-emerges to lead Tillingfold in John Parker's *The Village Cricket Match* (1978) and *Test Time at Tillingfold* (1979).

KEMPSHILL GOLF CLUB

E. C. Bentley's 'The Sweet Shot' from *Trent Intervenes* (1938)

Picturesque village golf links where detective Philip Trent is called to investigate the murder of Arthur Freer. Freer, an unpopular member, known for his habit of playing a solitary nine holes before breakfast six days a week 'even in the beastliest weather', has been found dead on the fairway of the second hole, his body singed, perhaps by a lightning strike—but there has been no lightning.

MIDHAMPTON CCC

Bruce Hamilton's *Pro* (1946)

County cricket club from the English midlands where all-rounder Edwin Lamb goes to ply his trade, achieving national note in 1923 when he devises 'Q-bowling': a style of attack involving in-swingers on leg stump. Lamb has cordial relations with his first captain Arthur Meadows ('It was not only that he was a very good captain; he had a real affection for the men who played under him, an affection that was warmly reciprocated') but falls out with his last Nigel le Mesurier, a toff and snob.

NEW YORK KNIGHTS

Bernard Malamud's *The Natural* (1952)

Down-at-heel baseball club joined by enigmatic left-fielder Roy Hobbs of the Oomoo Oilers. Hobbs, thirty-four, seems old to be starting out; his first attempt to make it in the major leagues was thwarted by a pistol-packing siren a decade earlier. But his powers are preternatural: his bat Wonderboy, carved from a tree split by lightning, hits the ball vast distances; on one occasion he leaps and pouches a runaway canary. Then come the hardships of form and fate, and the machinations of a conniving owner. Film version starring Robert Redford (1984).

CITY RUGBY LEAGUE CLUB

David Storey's *This Sporting Life* (1960)

Professional rugby club in anonymous northern industrial city in England where Arthur Machin, exempted from national service due to bad feet, goes to play. With support from his captain Frank Miles, Machin matures into 'the super ape beyond reproach': 'I began to enjoy running with the ball, really to want for it, lust for it, like I never had before, moving to openings and breaking through, and running with my elbows and knees high so that it really hurt to hold me.' But he is debilitated by personal misadventures, especially his crude affection for his landlady, Mrs Hammond, and the machinations of the clubs' backers, Weaver and Slomer.

STEEPLE SINDERBY WANDERERS

J. L. Carr's *How Steeple Sinderby Wanderers Won the FA Cup* (1975)

Inspired by Carr's season in 1930 with a struggling village soccer team South Milford White Rose, this is the fantasy of how a struggling village soccer team overcame all comers by implementing the postulations of the local school's Hungarian headmaster. Not surprisingly, they become the subject of national attention, allowing the team chairman Fangfoss to expatiate about Englishness on live television: 'Most Englishmen are sick to death of politicians and jacks in offices telling us who we are and what we want. The English are just what they always were—quiet, decent folk, saddled with parasites.'

PIN PALS

'Team Homer', episode 3F10 of *The Simpsons* (1996), written by Mike Sculley

'I'm tired of being a wanna-be league bowler,' announces Homer Simpson. 'I wanna be a league bowler!' Stupefied by ether and mistaking him for the Pillsbury Doughboy, C. Montgomery Burns stumps up the $500 registration fee for the Pin Pals, consisting of Homer, Otto, Moe and Apu. But when Burns regains his wits and decides that he wants to play in the team, its members are unimpressed. 'Call this an unfair generalisation if you must,' says Moe, 'but old people are no good at everything.'

AKIVA SOCIAL CLUB TABLE TENNIS TEAM

Howard Jacobson's *The Mighty Walzer* (1999)

Oliver Walzer, a timid youth but a ping-pong prodigy, is pushed by his father to join Manchester's leading Jewish team, and among the likes of Aishky Mistofsky, Twink Starr and Sheeny Waxman excels. Then Walzer's rites of passage are disrupted by a femme fatale ('Why would any normal man ever want to do anything but lose to Lorna Peachley?'), and he blows it ('Take me home Oliver. And then please leave me alone. Go and lose to someone else.').

MIAMI SHARKS

Oliver Stone's *Any Given Sunday* (1999)

Struggling member of the Association of Football Franchises of America coached by embittered, embattled Tony D'Amato (Al Pacino), torn between quarterbacks: grand old man Cap Rooney (Dennis Quaid) and intuitive but impulsive Steamin' Willie Beaman (Jamie Foxx). He favours the former, who embodies his conviction that the game 'has to be about more than winning', but is compelled by Rooney's injury to reach accord with the latter, who is in harmony with the win-at-all-costs attitude of Sharks' owner Christina Pagniacci (Cameron Diaz). The film features cameos from several gridiron greats, including Jim Brown and Dick Butkus; D'Amato's saturnine coaching nemesis in the climactic game against the Dallas Knights is Baltimore Colts legend Johnny Unitas.

TEN-GALLON HATS

The wide-brimmed, high-crowned ten-gallon cowboy hat is thought to be a Texan rendering of the sombrero favoured by Mexican *vaqueros*. The expression 'ten-gallon' owes nothing to the hat's imagined carrying capacity—even the largest would hold no more than four gallons of water—but to the Spanish word for braid: *galón*. *Vaqueros* commonly wreathed their sombreros with as many as ten braided hatbands, these becoming known as 'ten galón hats'. The hat was standardised in 1865 when John Batterson Stetson (1830–1906) of New Jersey opened a hatmaking factory in Philadelphia whose product became synonymous with quality and durability. He called his top of the line product 'Boss of the Plains', though it was soon colloquially known by his surname. The high-crowned hat found more willing admirers among the more diminutive stars of Westerns in the 1940s and 1950s, seeking to look taller.

TEN DEGREES OF HARDNESS

Devised by the German mineralogist Freidrich Mohs (1773–1839), the hardness scale is a key tool of materials science that ranks minerals according to their ability to make indented scratch marks in the mineral below them on the scale, from hardest (diamond) to softest (talc). Purely an ordinal ranking, it is here referenced with absolute hardness according to sclerometer.

RELATIVE HARDNESS	MATERIAL	ABSOLUTE HARDNESS
10	diamond	1500
9	corundum	400
8	topaz	200
7	quartz	100
6	orthoclase	72
5	apatite	48
4	fluorite	21
3	gypsum	9
2	calcite	3
1	talc	1

TEN PHONETIC DIGITS

0 Nadazero.............................nah-dah-zer-oh
1. Unaone.............................oo-nah-wun
2. Bissotwo.............................bee-soh-too
3. Terrathree.............................tey-ray-tree
4. Kartefour.............................kar-tay-fower
5. Pantafive.............................pan-tah-five
6. Soxisix.............................sok-see-six
7. Setteseven.............................say-tay-seven
8. Oktoeight.............................ok-tow-ait
9. Novenine.............................no-vey-nine

TEN GREAT ECONOMISTS

In this survey of the giants of his discipline by Joseph Schumpeter, posthumously published in 1951, economics is made to seem a science anything but dismal. *Ten Great Economists* is one of the most delightful and elegant books of its kind, not merely perceptive, but rhapsodic in the way their studies and reflections are evoked: this is the economist as hero, seer, explorer, messiah.

Karl Marx (1818–1883): 'In one important sense, Marxism is a religion. To the believer it presents, first, a system of ultimate ends that embody the meaning of life and are absolute standards by which to judge events and actions; and secondly, a guide to those ends which implies a plan of salvation and the indication of the evil from which mankind, or a chosen sector of mankind, is to be saved. We may specify still further: Marxist socialism also belongs to that subgroup which promises paradise on this side of the grave.'

Leon Walras (1834–1910): 'The fate of truth as well as beauty is a sad one on this earth...But this was not how he thought, and he never overcame the memory of struggles and failure. His autobiography ends with bitter words and he seems to have been given to bitter thoughts—thus an element of the tragic hovers over this life so outwardly quiet.'

Carl Menger (1840–1921): 'Anyone who understands the inner history of scientific progress will be aware of all the tactics employed in small circles in order to gain acceptance for new ideas. Menger did not know how that is done; and even if he had known, he lacked the means of conducting his own campaigns. But his powerful strength penetrated through all the jungles and triumphed over all the hostile armies.'

Alfred Marshall (1842–1924): 'He did not wish to frighten the layman, he wanted—strange ambition!—to be "read by businessmen". He was afraid, and justly, of setting an example which might induce people with a mathematical training to think that mathematics is all an economist needs...Yet one might wish that he had extended more encouragement to those who...were then beginning to espouse the cause of more exact economics...No science will ever progress if there are no runaways among its votaries.'

Vilfredo Pareto (1848–1923): 'The naive lover of modern social creeds and slogans must feel himself driven by clubs from Pareto's threshold; he reads what he is firmly resolved never to admit to be true and he reads it with a disconcerting wealth of practical examples.'

Eugen von Bohm-Bawerk (1851–1914): 'This gigantic massif of ideas is still too near us, the dust clouds of controversy are still too dense. For he was not only a creative mind but also a fighter—and to his last moments a live, effective force in our science.'

Frank Taussig (1859–1940): 'He was one of the first to realise that economic theory, like the theoretical part of any other subject, is not a storehouse of recipes or a philosophy, but a tool with which to analyse the economic patterns of real life. Hence the teacher's task consists of imparting...an art of formulating the questions to which we are to address the facts.'

Irving Fisher (1867–1947): 'Strange as it may seem in the case of a man of such monolithic purity of purpose, of such width of social sympathies, of such unqualified adherence to one of the ruling slogans of his day—stabilisation—he remained always outside of the current and always failed to convince either his contemporaries or the rising generations. But those pillars and arches will stand by themselves.'

Wesley Clair Mitchell (1874–1948): 'Here was a man who had the courage to say...that he had not all the answers; who went about this task without either haste or rest; who did not care to march along with his flags and brass bands; who was full of sympathy for mankind's fate, yet kept aloof from the market place; who taught us...what a scholar should be.'

J. M. Keynes (1883–1946): 'Keynes was no doubt too able an advocate ever to deny the obvious. To some extent, though probably to a small extent only, his success is precisely due to the fact that even in his boldest rushes he never left his flanks unguarded—as unwary critics of either his policies or his theories are apt to discover to their cost.'

TEN EXPRESSIONS OF ANAREITE ENGLISH

The vernacular of members of the Australian National Antarctic Research Expeditions contains expressions peculiar to those working in polar regions, some pre-existing, some of their own devising.

Big Eye	Insomnia attributed to lengthy periods of Antarctic daylight, first mentioned in Noel Barber's *The White Desert* (1958).
Degomble	To untangle or shake snow from clothing or a dog's coat.
Gashman	Expeditioner rostered for kitchen or cleaning duties. Also known as gash hand, housemouse or slushy.
Moop	One disoriented by the changing patterns of light and dark peculiar to polar regions (abbreviation for 'man out of phase'). Devised by ANARE scientist Edmund Widdows in the late 1950s.
RTAer	An expeditioner who is 'returning to Australia'.
Sago Snow	Snow that falls in small, hard, round balls, sometimes with a fluffy exterior; named by Shackleton in *The Heart of the Antarctic* (1909).
Turdicle	Frozen canine excrement.
Warmstore	A storage area kept at about the normal temperature of a refrigerator to prevent items from freezing altogether.
WYSSA	Code in communications to and from Australia for 'All my/our love, darling'. A relic of days when the expense of telex encouraged economy in words.
YIKLA	Code in communications to and from Australia for 'This is the life'.

TEN DEDICATIONS TO AUSTRALIAN POLITICAL WORKS

'I dedicate this book to my mother and to the people of Queensland.'
Joh Bjelke-Petersen, *Don't You Worry about That* (1990)

'To Doris, my wife, constant companion and loyal friend.'
Clyde Cameron, *The Cameron Diaries* (1990)

'For my son, Joseph.'
Paul Kelly, *The End of Certainty* (1992)

'To the men and women who made this story possible by their faith in the man whose life I shared.'
Dame Enid Lyons, *So We Take Comfort* (1965)

'For Frank Gladstone Menzies, CBE. Brother, counsellor and friend.'
Sir Robert Menzies, *Afternoon Light* (1967)

'For Graham Freudenberg, the real Boswell.'
Laurie Oakes, *Whitlam PM* (1973)

'This book is dedicated by special permission to Sir Winston Churchill, KG, OM, CH
whose courage and indomitable will saved the free world.'
Earle Page, *Truant Surgeon* (1963)

'To the tyrannical employer and the aggressive fighting trade unionist.'
W. G. Spence, *Australia's Awakening* (1909)

'Terry Counihan, Dinny O'Hearn, Peter Kerr
In memoriam.'
Don Watson, *Recollections of a Bleeding Heart* (2002)

'To my best appointment, Margaret Whitlam.'
Gough Whitlam, *The Whitlam Government* (1985)

DECANE

An alkane and hydrocarbon, one of the components of gasoline, containing ten carbon atoms. Represented by the chemical formula $C_{10}H_{22}$.

RICE IN TEN MINUTES

Requires half a cup of long grain white rice, two teaspoons of olive oil, salt and pepper. Bring two to three quarts of water to the boil, add rice, return to boil, and maintain for ten minutes in an uncovered saucepan. On tasting, the rice should be cooked through rather than soft. Drain, rinsing the rice with hot water, fluffing it with a fork. Mix the oil, salt and pepper to taste. Serves two.

TEN AUSTRALIAN PLACES WITH TRICKY PRONUNCIATIONS

Argyle, Western Australia . . . . AH-gyle
Argyle, New South Wales . . . . ah-GYLE
Collie, Western Australia . . . . COLL-ee
Collie, New South Wales . . . . COLL-eye
Eschol, Queensland . . . . ESH-ol
Eschol, New South Wales . . . . ESH-col
Eungella, Queensland . . . . YOUNG-gella
Eungella, New South Wales . . . . yoon-GHELLA
Glencoe, Queensland . . . . KLEN-ko
Glencoe, New South Wales . . . . GLEN-ko

TEN INDIAN TRAFFIC SIGNS

All motor vehicles prohibited

Compulsory sound horn

Bullock cart prohibited

Hand cart prohibited

School ahead

Cattle

Loose gravel

Falling rocks

Ferry

Barrier ahead

TEN 'GIRLS'

The Biograph Girl	Florence Lawrence (1886–1938)	Silent film siren
The Golden Girl of Pop	Kathy Kirby (1940–)	Singer
The Head Girl	Angela Rippon (1944–)	Newsreader
The It Girl	Clara Bow (1906–1965)	Actress, sex symbol
The Oomph Girl	Ann Sheridan (1915–1967)	Actress, pin-up girl
The Original Bathing Girl	Vera Steadman (1900–1966)	Actress, comedienne
The Original Box Office Girl	Mariane Michaelska (1898–1959)	Dancer, proponent of the shimmy
The Original Glamour Girl	Theodosia Goodman (1885–1955)	Actress, vamp
The Peekaboo Girl	Veronica Lake (1919–1973)	Actress, beauty
Poor Little Rich Girl	Gloria Vanderbilt (1924–)	Heiress, designer
The Sweater Girl	Lana Turner (1921–1995)	Actress, diva

TEN PSEUDONYMS USED BY DANIEL DEFOE

Solomon Waryman — Miranda Meanwell — Sir Malcontent Chagrin — Sir Fopling Tittle-Tattle — Jeremiah Dry-Boots — Obadiah Blue Hat — Boatswain Trinkolo — Theophilus Lovewit — Anglipolski of Lithuania — Count Kidneyface

Defoe (1660–1731) is believed to have used as many as 198 pseudonyms

FOWLER METHOD

System for casting reinforced concrete wall panels using an elevated flat metal table tilted after the concrete's maturity to a vertical position, ready for transport and bolting together. Devised in the 1920s by structural engineer T. W. Fowler (1875–1942). His plant, taken over in 1944 by the Victorian Housing Commission and relocated to Holmesglen, was integral to postwar public housing.

KENNY METHOD

Approach to the treatment of infantile paralysis (poliomyelitis) in which rehabilitation is expedited by stimulation and re-education of the paralysed muscles. Devised by Australian nurse Elizabeth Kenny (1880–1952), daughter of an Irish veterinary surgeon, who between 1933 and 1938 opened a string of clinics round Australia following her teachings. Opposed by the medical profession and stymied by a royal commission, she relocated to the United States in 1941 and was recognised at once as a medical innovator.

METHOD ACTING

Application of natural rules and laws to the theatre to promote the verisimilitude of acting performance with life. Promoted by Russian acting teacher Konstantin Stanislavski (1863–1938), later popularised by Lee Strasberg (1901–1982) among a generation of American actors including Paul Newman, Al Pacino, Marilyn Monroe, Jane Fonda, James Dean, Dustin Hoffman, Eli Wallach, Eva Marie Saint, Robert DeNiro, Jill Clayburgh, Jack Nicholson and Steve McQueen.

MÉTHODE CHAMPENOISE

Costly, labour-intensive but time-honoured production technique in the manufacture of sparkling wine that involves careful cellaring and the promotion of a second fermentation in the bottle. Traditionally identified with the Champagne region of France, 200 kilometres north-east of Paris. Anagram of: 'Men-made hooch? It's pee!'

MONTESSORI METHOD

Educational method championed by Italian doctor Maria Montessori (1870–1952) promoting a holistic approach to learning in which social skills, emotional growth and physical co-ordination are given as much attention as cognitive preparation. Montessorri enjoined teachers to refrain from 'obtrusive interference', and believed: 'Human teachers can only help the great work that is being done, as servants help the master.'

NEWTON'S METHOD

Method delineated in *Philosophiae Naturalis Principia Mathematica* (1687) by English mathematician Isaac Newton (1643–1727) to approximate roots of functions; equivalently, solutions to equations of the form f(x)=0. Also described by Newton's contemporary Joseph Raphson (1648–1715) in *Analysis Aequationum* (1690), and thus sometimes refered to as the Newton–Raphson Method.

POTTER-DELPRAT METHOD

Process for the treatment of rock crushings using bubbles stimulated by acid, salt or other chemical to float ore to the surface, developed in Broken Hill in 1903. The synthesis of two rival processes developed by a Melbourne brewer, Charles Potter (1859–1908), and the general manager of BHP, Guillaume Delprat (1856–1937).

RHYTHM METHOD

Contraceptive practice, also known as natural family planning and periodic abstinence, that prevents pregnancy by avoiding intercourse around the time of the woman's ovulation, which is determined by the use of a calendar, a thermometer to measure body temperature, and a kit that tests the thickness of cervical mucus. Described in *The British Museum Is Falling Down* (1965) by David Lodge (b. 1935) as leading to 'three weeks of patient graph-plotting, followed by a few nights of frantic love-making, which rapidly petered out in exhaustion and renewed suspense'.

THE METHOD

'A kind of third-degree psychological investigation applied to the souls of one's friends' involving prepared questions and a prosecutorial approach devised at Cambridge University by Bloomsbury contemporaries Lytton Strachey (1880–1932) and Leonard Woolf (1880–1969).

In *Sowing* (1960), the first volume of his autobiography, Woolf describes it as inspired by Socrates, Henry James and G. E. Moore: 'It was intended to reveal to us, and incidentally to the victim, what he was really like; the theory was that by imparting to all concerned the deeper psychological truths, personal relationships would be much improved.'

TOMATIS METHOD
Approach to the treatment of attention deficit disorder, autism and dyslexia involving emphasis on the development of listening skills. According to its French originator Dr Alfred Tomatis (1920–2001): 'To learn, you have to be able to listen.' Tomatis outlined the principles of what he called Audio-Psycho-Phonology (APP) in *L'Oreille et le Langage* (1963) and *Education et Dyslexie* (1972).

WORLD WAR II MILITARY CASUALTIES AMONG TEN BRITISH ALLIES

After resigning from office in April 1955, Sir Winston Churchill asked his private secretary to arrange for a collation of statistics regarding military and civilian deaths during World War II. British and Dominion deaths were sharply lower than those sustained during World War I—373,372 compared with 779,468—but those among ten Allied countries far higher.

Belgium	22,651
China	1,500,000
Denmark	6400
France	245,000
Greece	253
Netherlands	230,177
Norway	1598
Sweden	3318
USA	520,433
USSR	4,500,000

The total, 7,029,830, was considerably greater than the 1,174,595 aggregated in World War I. Enemy deaths were also far greater, 8,513,378 versus 3,751,466.

TEN SAINTS IDENTIFIED WITH AFFLICTIONS

St Peregrine Laziosi	Cancer
St Vitus	Epilepsy
St Fiacre	Haemorrhoids
St Dympna	Mental illness
St Giles	Paralysis
St Hubert	Rabies
St Anthony	Skin disease
St Blaise	Throat infections
St Appollonia	Toothache

TEN HOURS' BILL

The culmination of forty-five years of British legislative reform following the Industrial Revolution. It followed the Factory Act (1802), limiting to twelve hours the shift of an apprentice child, and the Factory Act (1833), which prohibited the employment of children under nine and limited shifts for children aged nine to thirteen to eight hours while providing for their mandatory education for at least two hours a day. What became known as the Ten Hours' Bill (1847), advocated with consuming zeal by the philanthropist and MP Lord Shaftesbury (1801–1885), restricted the working day for women and children to that time, and became the basis for future reforms designed to consolidate its supervision.

TEN MICHELANGELO ANTONIONI FILMS

Love in the City (1953), *The Outcry* (1957), *L'Avventura* (1960), *La Notte* (1961), *Eclipse* (1962), *Red Desert* (1964), *Blowup* (1966), *Zabriskie Point* (1970), *The Passenger* (1975), *Identification of a Woman* (1982).

'Men are men, and this is a game for men.' Thus Richmond ruckman Jack Dyer aka 'Captain Blood' in *The Wild Men of Football* (1968), which remains the ur-text of Australian rules football books, painting a vivid portrait of the game's halcyon period of uninhibited violence. Here are ten acts from the era as recorded by their perpetrators and Dyer (and his amanuensis Brian Hansen).

Mopsy Fraser
Richmond (124 games) 1945–1952
'When I realised a collision was inevitable I put my elbow up to guard against the shirtfront. CRACK! The bone in my forearm exploded and the sound of breaking carried across the ground…I had to go off, and as I walked round the boundary a spectator screamed: "Serves you right, Fraser; it's a pity it wasn't your bleeding neck." As one we both swung hooks at the bloke. I threw a right and Norm threw a left. They exploded side by side on his jaw and we continued our walk.'

Ron Barassi Jnr
Melbourne (204 games) 1953–1964; Carlton (49 games) 1965–1969
'Be it good or bad, my tongue and its use is part of my natural game and I haven't the time to spend altering my style.' Charging through a pack against North, he crashed into the ferocious Albert Mantello: 'Get out of the way, dago!' he snarled. Mantello smirked: 'You should talk, Barassi!'

John Coleman
Essendon (98 games) 1949–1954
'In fact, I feel safer on the ground where I know the opposition is coming from. But those characters over the fence are a different matter. You don't worry so much about the bottles, but there was a jagged piece of bitumen thrown at me the other day. Luckily it bounced before it hit me. If it hadn't I guess it would have sliced off

my kneecap…I wouldn't go after seeing one citizen smash a bottle on a fence and jab the broken end into a man's face.'

Murray Weideman

Collingwood (159 games) 1953–1963

'Unless a team has an enforcer, its players will be victimised and put off their game by the ever-present hit-and-run bash artist. The only way to subdue the sly-knuckle man is to flatten him with a legitimately directed shoulder or rib-busting shirtfront, delivered at top speed. Victorians still like to see blood spilt on the turf, particularly if the victim is a member of the opposition, particularly if it is someone like me.'

Carl Ditterich

St Kilda (203 games) 1963–1972, 1976–78; Melbourne (82 games) 1973–1975, 1979–1980

'In his first game he clashed with Mr Big of football, Ron Barassi, and in a moment of feckless youth advised: "Step aside grandad."…He was the target from the opening bounce and was jostled, punched and goaded throughout the day and even the spectators joined in and one threw a can of filth over him.'

Ted Whitten

Footscray (321 games) 1951–1970

'Lou [Richards] came bursting from a pack chattering away to himself and looking for all the world like a monkey. WHAM! I slammed into him full pelt, and my shoulder rammed his jaw. It was the first time I ever saw him stop talking…His jaw was dislocated but he was still able to mumble: "Your turn will come Whitten."

Bobby Skilton

South Melbourne (238 games) 1956–1971

'Charlie Sutton…hurtled at Skilton from the back pocket and the South selectors shuddered as the youngster refused to change course. As the fatal crash seemed inevitable, young Skilton gave a twist to the left, missed Sutton by a whisker, steadied and banged for goal. That was it.'

John Peck
Hawthorn (213 games) 1954–1966
'The huge crowd was stunned to see Peck hurtle from the ground swinging a ferocious uppercut which was perfection in timing. It landed so squarely and firmly on South Australian Brian Sawley's jaw that it lifted him off the ground. Sawley crashed on his back without a muscle twitching.'

Norm Smith
Melbourne (210 games) 1935–1948, Fitzroy (17 games) 1949–1950
'I have always been fiery. Yet perhaps some of that fire could have played a part in the great success of the club. WEAK MEN CAN'T WIN PREMIERSHIPS.'

Jack Dyer
Richmond (312 games) 1931–1949
'Suddenly,' [recalled Mopsy Fraser,] 'Jack saw a opportunity to settle an old score. Alby Pannam stuck his head out. Dyer thundered in and I saw Pannam's legs start to shake, he could never have gotten out of the way. Suddenly [Richmond's] Bill Morris wandered across the line of fire, saw Jack too late, and yelled: "Aww, nooo." BOOM!'

TEN PSEUDONYMS USED BY VOLTAIRE

Genest Ramponeau — Dominico Zapata — Major Kaiserling — Dr Good Natur'd Wellwisher — Dom Calmet — Don Apueleius Risorius — George Aronger Dardelle — Abbe Tamponet — Abbe Maudit — Mr Sherloc

Voltaire, of course, is itself a pseudonym, for Francois-Marie Arouet (1694–1778)

TEN COMMON SYMBOLS IN CIRCUIT DIAGRAMS

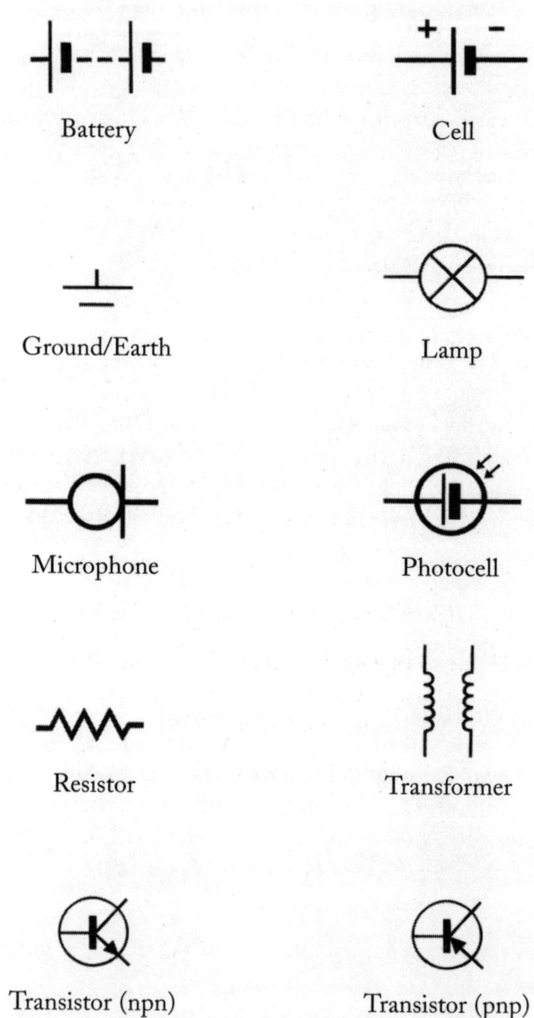

TEN IMPRESSIONS OF CHURCHILL

'He is a young man who will go far if he doesn't overbalance.'
Cecil Rhodes (1901)

'First impression: restless, almost intolerably so, without capacity for sustained or unexcited labour, egotistical, bumptious, shallow-minded and reactionary, but with a certain personal magnetism, great pluck and some originality, not of intellect but of character. More of the American speculator than the English aristocrat.'
Beatrice Webb (1903)

'Napoleonic in audacity. Cromwellian in thoroughness.'
Jacky Fisher (1912)

'Churchill is a good judge in every matter that does not concern himself. There, his judgement is hopeless, and he is sure to come to a big crash in time.'
Lord Beaverbrook (1925)

'When he becomes engrossed in his subject he strides up and down the room with his head thrust forward and his thumbs in the armholes of his waistcoat, as if he were trying to keep pace with his own eloquence.'
James Scrymgeour-Wedderburn (1928)

'He fits all the roles with such exceeding facility that his lack of political stability is at once explained.'
Aneurin Bevan (1929)

'Winston would go up to his Creator and say that he would very much like to meet His Son, about Whom he had heard a great deal and, if possible, would like to call on the Holy Ghost. Winston *loved* meeting people.'
David Lloyd George (1937)

'Always expecting rabbits to come out of empty hats.'
Lord Wavell (1943)

'His passion for the combative renders him insensitive to the gentle gradations of the human mind.'
Harold Nicolson (1945)

'The man who may be the wrecker of the Tory Party, but was certainly the saviour of the civilised world.'
Henry Channon (1952)

TEN TRADITIONAL METHODS OF DESTROYING A VAMPIRE

Staking — Beheading# — Sunlight — Cremation —
Piercing with a sword^ — Immersion in water —
Drenching in garlic and holy water — Touching with a crucifix* —
Trapping in the grave — Extraction of heart

#Avoid blood splattering ^Sword must be blessed
*Recent vampires only

THE TENTH ELEMENT

Neon, the tenth element, from the Greek word for new, was first extracted from liquid air by Scottish chemist William Ramsay (1852–1916) and his assistant Morris Travers (1872–1961) in 1898, as part of researches that also isolated three other inert gases: helium, krypton and xenon. Ramsay, who had six years earlier discovered argon in work with the physicist Lord Rayleigh, was the Nobel laureate for chemistry in 1904, and knighted in 1906.

TEN ANIMALS THAT SHARE A MALE

elks* — fur seals* — Hamadryas baboons* — mountain sheep* —
pheasants# — prairie chickens# — red grouse# — wild horses* —
wrens# — yellow-bellied marmots*

*Mammal #Bird

TEN TESTS

AMES TEST

Determining if a chemical is a mutagen (an agent that causes mutation), based on the assumption that any substance that is mutagenic may also prove carcinogenic. Its developer, geneticist Bruce Ames (b. 1928), remains Professor of Biochemistry and Molecular Biology at Berkeley and a Senior Scientist at Children's Hospital Oakland Research Institute, but now plays down alarms about potential carcinogens: 'We are the healthiest we have ever been in human history.'

THE ELECTRIC KOOL-AID ACID TEST (1968)

Heavily embroidered account by journalist Tom Wolfe (b. 1930) of a cross-country counter-cultural journey by novelist Ken Kesey (1935–2001) and his acid-dropping acolytes the Merry Pranksters in their multicoloured bus Furthur. With *The Kandy-Kolored Tangerine-Flake Streamline Baby* (1965), *The Pump House Gang* (1968) and *Radical Chic and Mau-Mauing the Flak Catchers* (1970), it exemplified the so-called New Journalism.

EYSENCK PERSONALITY TEST

Popular psychological inventory devised by prolific German theorist and researcher Hans Eysenck (1916–1997) to map the interaction of what he called the two supertraits: Extroversion-Introversion, and Neuroticism. Explained in *The Biological Basis of Personality* (1967); revisited in *Psychology Is about People* (1972).

ISHIHARA TEST

The standard test for colour-blindness, employing a series of pseudoisochromatic plates on which numbers or letters are printed in dots of primary colours surrounded by dots of other colours. The figures, discernible by individuals with normal vision, present difficulties for the colour-blind. Devised by the Japanese ophthalmologist Shinobu Ishihara (1879–1963).

MANTOUX TEST

For almost a century, the most robust and effective means of ascertaining a tubercular infection. The tuberculin—a derivative of tubercle bacillus—is injected intradermally. A red area appearing within the next three days signifies a recent exposure to the disease and the need for further testing. Named for its discoverer, the French physician Charles Mantoux (1877–1947).

MYERS–BRIGGS TEST

Popular psychometric test, widely used in recruiting and management consultancy, that measures a respondent's preferences using four basic scales with opposite poles: extraversion/introversion; sensate/intuitive; thinking/feeling; judging/perceiving. Inspired by the book *Psychological Types* (1921) by Carl Jung, the test was developed by Isabel Briggs Myers (1897–1979), a political scientist from Swarthmore College, in collaboration with her mother.

RORSCHACH TEST

Devised by Swiss psychiatrist Hermann Rorschach (1884–1922), a disciple of Eugen Bleuler, this classic psychodiagnostic tool, seeking the responses of patients to inkblot images so that they might be interpreted according to a predetermined system, was first outlined publicly in *Psychodiagnostik* (1921). There are actually only ten inkblots, and findings are based as much on the patient's response to the test as their remarks about the images. The test's popularity peaked in the 1960s; it is now seldom used.

STANFORD–BINET TEST

A standard intelligence test for the assessment of children adapted for use in the United States from the French Binet–Simon Scale by researchers at California's Stanford University. Its originators were the French psychologists Alfred Binet (1857–1911) and Théodore Simon (1873–1961).

TURING TEST

A benchmark for artificial intelligence set by the gifted British mathematician Alan Turing (1912–1954), famous for heading Allied code-breaking activities at Bletchley Park during World War II. In a

1950 contribution to *Mind,* 'Computing Machinery and Intelligence', Turing asked: Can a Machine Think? Believing that one day a machine would, he mused: 'If a computer could think, how could we tell?' His proposition was that a computer could be said to be thinking if its responses were indistinguishable from that of a human. In 1990, the maverick American scientist Dr Hugh Loebner agreed with The Cambridge Center for Behavioral Studies to endow a contest based on the Turing Test to the extent of $100,000 and a Gold Medal.

WASSERMANN TEST

The standard method of detecting syphilis in humans devised by the German bacteriologist August von Wassermann (1866–1925). A complement fixation test is used to detect antibodies to the syphilis organism treponema; a positive reaction indicates the presence of antibodies and therefore syphilis infection.

SONGS COMPOSED FOR THE CAMPAIGNS OF TEN US PRESIDENTS

'Keep Cool and Keep Coolidge'. . . . . Calvin Coolidge
'The Boss of the Nation' . . . . Grover Cleveland
'Keep the Ball A-Rolling' . . . . Ulysses S. Grant
'Tippecanoe and Tyler Too' . . . . William Henry Harrison
'Hurrah for Hayes and Honest Ways' . . . . Rutherford B. Hayes
'The Man for Uncle Sam' . . . . Herbert Hoover
'Old Rosin the Beau'. . . . . James K. Polk
'Goodbye Teddy, You Must March, March, March'. Teddy Roosevelt
'Get in Line for Big Bill Taft' . . . . William Howard Taft
'I Think We've Got Another Washington and Wilson Is His Name' . . . . Woodrow Wilson

THE NUMBERS ONE TO TEN IN TEN LANGUAGES

	1	2	3	4	5	6	7	8	9	10
Afrikaans	een	twee	drie	vier	vyf	ses	sewe	agt	nege	tien
French	un	deux	trois	quatre	cinq	six	sept	huit	neuf	dix
German	eins	zwei	drei	vier	fünf	sechs	sieben	acht	neun	zehn
Greek	éna	dhío	tría	téssera	pénde	éksi	eftá	oxtó	ennéa	dhéka
Italian	uno	due	tre	quattro	cinque	sei	sette	otto	nove	dieci
Portuguese	um	dois	três	quatro	cinco	seis	sete	oito	nove	dez
Russian	odín	dva	tri	chety're	pyat'	shest'	sem'	vósem'	dévyat'	désyat'
Scots	ane	twa	thrie	fower	fyve	sax	seiven	aicht	nyne	ten
Spanish	uno	dos	tres	cuatro	cinco	seis	siete	ocho	nueve	diez
Swedish	en	två	tre	fyra	fem	sex	sju	åtta	nio	tio
Welsh	un	dau	tri	pedwar	pump	chwech	saith	wyth	naw	deg

TEN-MINUTE RULE BILLS

A type of Private Member's Bill in Britain's House of Commons, introduced by backbench MPs on their own initiative with a speech of no more than ten minutes' duration, usually as public business commences on most Tuesdays and Wednesdays. MPs must give fifteen days' notice to the Public Bill Office of their intention to present such a bill and only one may be introduced on any one day. Seldom does the government permit the progress of a Ten-Minute Rule Bill to law, but opportunities for their introduction are coveted as a means of obtaining publicity for particular issues; immediately after Question Time, the house is usually close to full. MPs have been known to sleep overnight in the PBO antechamber three weeks prior to their intended date of presentation in order to claim the opportunity by being first through the door. Conservative MP David Davis has described Ten-Minute Rule Bills as a 'valuable method of allowing backbenchers to express a view on a subject that they feel is important'.

WORLD'S TEN TALLEST WATERFALLS

1.	Angel Falls, Venezuela	979m (3212ft)
2.	Tugela, South Africa	948m (3110ft)
3.	Utigord, Norway	800m (2625ft)
4.	Mongefossen, Norway	774m (2540ft)
5.	Yosemite, USA	739m (2425ft)
6.	Ostre Mardola, Norway	657m (2154ft)
7.	Tyssestrengane, Norway	646m (2120ft)
8.	Kukenaom, Venezuela	610m (2000ft)
9.	Sutherland, New Zealand	580m (1904ft)
10.	Kjellfossen, Norway	561m (1841ft)

TEN PARAGRAPHS CONCERNING 10 DOWNING STREET

1. Number 10 Downing Street, SW1, in the City of Westminster is not the official residence of the British prime minister, but the official residence of the First Lord of Treasury, an archaic office filled for the last century by the prime minister. Since renovation in the 1940s, the house has been essentially an office, with the former servants quarters turned into a residential space, although Tony Blair and family reside in what is officially the apartment of the Chancellor of the Exchequer at 11 Downing Street, while bachelor Chancellor Gordon Brown lives in the quarters at number 10, the former being slightly more commodious.

2. Over time, prime ministers have had varying degrees of involvement with the building. Some, including the Duke of Wellington (1769–1852), have refused to live there at all, on grounds of its size; others have already had private London residences at which they have preferred to remain. Only since the premiership of Arthur Balfour (1848–1930) between 1902 and 1905 has the office holder tended to live there full time.

3. Downing Street itself, a cul-de-sac off the west side of Whitehall, was built in about 1680 by George Downing MP (c. 1623–1684). Downing, a crony of Oliver Cromwell's who became his intelligence chief, had switched his allegiance to the monarchy after the Restoration. A portrait of Downing still hangs in the entrance hall.

4. The residence was a gift of George II to Sir Robert Walpole (1676–1745), the first British prime minister in the modern sense and still the longest-serving, in 1732. Walpole accepted on condition that the gift was made to the office of First Lord of Treasury rather than to himself. The last private resident of the building was a Mr Chicken.

5. The house was originally 5 Downing Street, renumbering occurring in 1779. Numbers 11 and 12 Downing Street—reserved

respectively for the Chancellor and Chief Whip—were acquired by the crown about two hundred years ago. The three official residences are the only houses to survive from George Downing's original strip.

6. Over time, 10 Downing Street has merged into the house immediately behind it, a larger and more handsome terrace facing Horseguards Parade. This was built around 1677 for the Countess of Lichfield, Charles II's daughter, but its owner Count Bothmor died in 1732 when the original gift to Walpole was made, and the two residences were connected by architect William Kent.

7. Between 1766 and 1774, the premierships of the Duke of Grafton (1735–1805) and Lord North (1732–1792), extensive repair work was undertaken. A black and white chequerboard floor was laid in the entrance hall; the lamp above the door and the lion's head doorknocker also date from around this time.

8. In 1796, during the premiership of William Pitt (1759–1806), the Cabinet Room was created by knocking a wall down and inserting columns to carry the extra span. Since the 1860s, however, there has also been a Cabinet Room across the road in the palatial Foreign Office building designed by George Gilbert Scott.

9. Nothing has been rushed about 10 Downing Street. It did not obtain electric lighting until 1894. Telephones followed. Computer cabling was not introduced until ten years ago.

10. Security, too, has only recently become a preoccupation. Although the entrance to 10 Downing Street is guarded night and day by a policeman, and its front door can only be opened from the inside, it was not until 1989 that Margaret Thatcher had heavy iron gates installed where Downing Street met Whitehall, sealing it from traffic altogether, and discontinued the custom of allowing children to stand on the steps and have photographs taken. After the house was damaged in a mortar attack by the Provisional IRA in August 1991, Prime Minister John Major was forced to relocate temporarily to Admiralty House.

TEN CLASSIC TRICK QUESTIONS

i) What was Iran called before it was Persia?
ii) How much dirt is there in a hole three metres deep, six metres long and four metres wide?
iii) Who was the last captain of England to go through a tour of Australia undefeated?
iv) Which male body part swells to ten times its normal size when stimulated?
v) Some months have thirty-one days, others have thirty days. How many have twenty-eight days?
vi) Which Australian city was named after Thomas Townsend?
vii) Which popular cheese is made backwards?
viii) How quickly can you find out what is unusual about this paragraph? It looks so ordinary that you would think that nothing was wrong with it at all, and in fact, nothing is. But it is unusual. Why? If you study it and think about it you may find out, but I am not going to assist you in any way. You must do it without coaching. No doubt if you work at it for long, it will dawn on you. I don't know. Now, go to work and try your luck.
ix) When did Coventry City last win the FA Cup?

Answers on p. 56.

FATES OF TEN NOTORIOUS AMERICAN OUTLAWS

Jesse James	Murdered for bounty, 1882
Johnny Torrio	Seriously wounded/retired, 1925
'Bugs' Moran	Shot during St Valentine's Day Massacre, 1929
'Dutch' Schultz	Shot by enemies, died of wounds, 1930
Al Capone	Sentenced to jail for tax evasion, 1931
'Machine Gun' Kelly	Captured, 1934
'Pretty Boy' Floyd	Shot and killed by law enforcers, 1934
John Dillinger	Shot and killed by law enforcers, 1934
'Baby Face' Nelson	Shot and killed by law enforcers, 1934
'Lucky' Luciano	Deported to Italy, 1946

TEN BILDUNGSROMANS

Tom Jones (1749) . . . . Henry Fielding
Wilhelm Meister's Apprenticeship (1775) . . Johann Wolfgang von Goethe
Heinrich von Ofterdingen (1799) . . . . . . Novalis (Friedrich Leopold)
Emma (1816) . . . . Jane Austen
David Copperfield (1849) . . . . Charles Dickens
Green Henry (1855) . . . . Gottfried Keller
The Way of All Flesh (1903) . . . . Samuel Butler
Portrait of the Artist As a Young Man (1915) . . . . James Joyce
Demian (1919) . . . . Herman Hesse
The Magic Mountain (1924) . . . . Thomas Mann

TEN COUNTRIES THAT BORDER BRAZIL

Uruguay — Argentina — Paraguay — Bolivia — Peru — Colombia — Venezuela — Guyana — Surinam — French Guiana

AVERAGE ERECT PENIS LENGTH OF TEN CREATURES

Mosquito . . . . 0.0254 cm (1/100 inch)
Cat . . . . 1.905 cm (3/4 inch)
Gorilla . . . . 5.08 cm (2")
Man . . . . 15.24 cm (6")
Pig . . . . 46–51 cm (18–20")
Rhinoceros . . . . 61 cm (2')
Horse . . . . 76 cm (2'6")
Bull . . . . 91 cm (3')
Elephant . . . . 152–183 cm (5–6')
Humpback whale . . . . 304.8 cm (10')

J. J. Audubon

John James Audubon (1785–1851)

George Cruikshank

George Cruikshank (1792–1878)

L. David

Jacques Louis David (1748–1825)

EUG. DELACROIX.

Eugene Delacroix (1798–1863)

TG.

Thomas Gainsborough (1727–1788)

W Hogarth

William Hogarth (1697–1764)

Rembrandt. f. 1650

Rembrandt van Rijn (1606–1669)

J. Reynolds

Sir Joshua Reynolds (1723–1792)

Tiepolo

Giovanni Tiepolo (1727–1804)

Turner

Joseph Turner (1775–1851)

POLONIUS' TEN PRECEPTS TO LAERTES

1. Give thy thoughts no tongue / Or any unproportioned thought his act
2. Be thou familiar, but by no means vulgar
3. The friends thou hast, and their adoption tried / Grapple them unto thy soul with hoops of steel
4. But do not dull thy palm with entertainment / Of each new hatch'd, unfledg'd comrade
5. Beware of entrance to a quarrel, but, being in, / Bear that th' opposed may beware of thee
6. Give every man thy ear, but few thy voice
7. Take each man's censure, but reserve thy judgment
8. The apparel oft proclaims the man
9. Neither a borrower nor a lender be
10. This above all: to thine own self be true

WORLD'S TEN GREATEST DEPRESSIONS

		Metres/Feet below Sea Level
1.	Dead Sea, Jordan–Israel	395m (1296ft)
2.	Turfan Depression, China	153m (505ft)
3.	Qattara Depression, Egypt	132m (436ft)
4.	Poluostrov Mangyshlak, Kazakhstan	131m (433ft)
5.	Danakil Depression, Ethiopia	116m (383ft)
6.	Death Valley, California	86m (282ft)
7.	Salton Sink, California	71m (235ft)
8.	Zapadnyy Chink Ustyurta, Kazakhstan	70m (230ft)
9.	Prikaspiyskaya Nizmennost, Russia–Kazakhstan	67m (220ft)
10.	Ozera Sarykamysh, Uzbekistan–Turkmenistan	45m (148ft)

TEN WORKS NOT WRITTEN BY SAMUEL COLERIDGE

During the summer of 1796, the English poet and critic Samuel Taylor Coleridge (1772–1834) recorded in his notebooks elaborate plans for his future literary endeavours including the following:

~ Essay on Rev. William Bowles (poet, author of *Sonnets*, 'Written chiefly on Picturesque Spots, during a Tour')
~ An epic poem 'The Origin of Evil'
~ Essay 'Strictures on William Godwin' (political philosopher, author of *Political Justice*)
~ 'Egonomist, a metaphysical Rhapsody'
~ Essay on Pantisocracy (the self-governing pastoral social model of which Coleridge was an advocate)
~ Essay on marriage ('in opposition to French principles')
~ Essay on Jakob Boehme (German mystic and Gnostic philosopher, author of *The Life Which Is above Sense*)
~ A poem 'Escapes from Misery' ('Halo round the Candle—Sigh visible')
~ Essay on the 'Reveries' of Emanuel Swedenborg (Swedish scientist, philosopher and theologian)
~ 'Wild Poem on Maniac'

In common with much of Coleridge's oeuvre, none was started, let alone completed. Considering his flair for visionary works that remained visions in his autobiographical *Literaria Biographia* written twenty years later, Coleridge explained: 'By what I have effected am I to be judged by my fellow men, what I could have done is a question for my own conscience.'

BORN IN THE YEAR TEN

10 B.C. ~ Claudius (died A.D. 54): Roman Emperor 41–A.D. 54.
A.D. 10 ~ Hero of Alexandria (died A.D. 70): Greek engineer famous for designing the first steam engine, the aeolipile.

THE UPPER TEN

One of the first phrases expressing the idea of an American elite, originated about 160 years ago by the journalist and short-story writer Nathaniel Parker Willis (1806–1867) to describe 'the upper ten thousand' in New York society. It was originally cited in the inaugural edition of the *Dictionary of Americanisms* (1848) by Willis' friend John Russell Bartlett (1805–1886).

TWO CHARLES XS

CHARLES X of Sweden (1622–1660), a member of the House of Wittelsbach, succeeded to the throne in June 1654 after the abdication of his cousin Queen Christina. Within a year he was waging an unsuccessful war on Poland, but avoided more serious consequences by turning on Denmark and securing the advantageous Treaty of Roskilde (1658) extending Sweden's frontier to the sea.

CHARLES X of France (1757–1836), after twenty-five years in exile following the French Revolution, returned to France with the Bourbon restoration and succeeded his brother Louis XVIII in September 1824. The severity of the advice of his chief minister Jules Armand de Polignac—who recommended restricting suffrage, dissolving the chamber of deputies and revoking the freedom of the press—was the *casus belli* of the July revolution, from which he fled after abdicating in favour of his grandson, the Comte de Chambord. He was succeeded instead by the Duc d'Orléans, whom he had appointed Lieutenant-General of France, and who reigned as Louis Philippe.

Answers to p. 50

1. Iran. 2. None; it is a hole. 3. Captain Cook. 4. The iris. 5. All of them. 6. Sydney; Thomas Townsend was Lord Sydney. 7. Edam—'made' backwards. 8. The paragraph is a lipogram: that is, it does not contain an 'e'. 9. Coventry City have never won the FA Cup (from Communist Quiz, 'Monty Python's Flying Circus').

TEN JOHISMS

Sir Johannes Bjelke-Petersen (1911–), the populist premier of Queensland from August 1968 to December 1987, was a Lutheran pastor's son turned peanut farmer who continued to sound like one for the duration of his forty-year political career—something intrinsic to his appeal in a state suspicious of city slickers and southern sophisticates. Something of his flair for testing the limits of language is evinced by the following:

'I don't want to be political but you can't trust the ALP.'

'Australia is bankrupt. It is even worse than that.'

'I mark special sections and my favourite verses.'
On motel Bibles.

'I am the flying peanut.'
After obtaining his pilot licence.

'As wealthy as Arab oil sheiks.'
Of Aborigines.

'The forty-hour week has given the opportunity to many to while away their time in hotels.'

'Uganda had first choice.'
Asked why he, not Idi Amin, was Queensland's premier.

'Like a school of whales intent on committing political suicide.'
Of the Fraser government when it wanted to declare the Cairns section of the Great Barrier Reef a marine park.

'We won't be able to sit on uranium firstly because it would not be right and secondly because it would be wrong as far as we are concerned.'

'That's all right. There are no votes south of Coolangatta.'
Told that some of his remarks occasioned southern mirth.

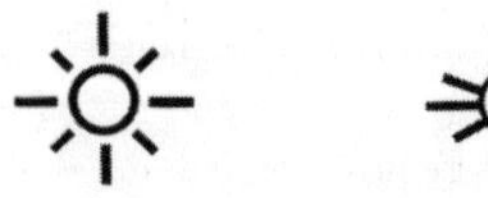

Brightness control

Flashbulb

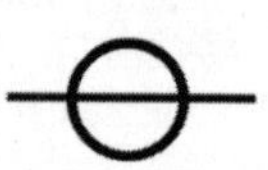

Focal plane

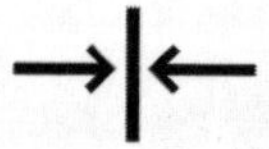

Focus

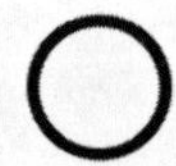

Maximal aperture

Minimal aperture

Suitable for photographing in cloudy weather

Suitable for photographing in sunlight

Zoom

COLOMBO PLAN

An agreement for cooperative development between countries of south and south-east Asia devised and agreed at a meeting of Commonwealth foreign ministers in Colombo in January 1950. Initial signatories were Afghanistan, Australia, Bhutan, Burma, Canada, Ceylon (Sri Lanka), India, Indonesia, Japan, Cambodia, Laos, the Maldives, Malaya (Malaysia), Nepal, New Zealand, Pakistan, Persia (Iran), Philippines, Singapore, South Korea, Thailand, the United Kingdom and United States.

DALTON PLAN

A progressive educational philosophy advocated by Helen Parkhurst (1887–1959) in her *Education on the Dalton Plan* (1922). Inspired by her experiences in a Wisconsin log-cabin school, Parkhurst founded a schoolhouse in Dalton, Massachusetts in 1916. The scheme involved students undertaking monthly projects in each subject, set according to individual capability, at their own speed, with minimal supervision. Classes were called as necessary; co-operation was encouraged; school rooms were called 'laboratories'. 'It is no longer school,' claimed Parkhurst. 'It is life.' The Children's University School that Parkhurst established in New York in 1919 still exists. Dalton Plan schools also operate in Australia, Chile, Czech Republic, Korea, the Netherlands, Taiwan and the United Kingdom.

DEATH ON THE INSTALMENT PLAN

Published in 1936, the second semi-autobiographical novel by Louis-Ferdinand Destouches aka Celine (1894–1961), a sequel to *Journey to the End of the Night* (1932). It continues the black, bleak story of Celine's alter ego Ferdinand Bardamu, introducing him to the inventor, adventurer and embezzler Courtial des Pereires and his grand ballooning plans. Notable for its grim aperçus, such as: 'Destiny eats prayers like a toad eats flies.'

DER PLAN

Dusseldorf *neu deutsche welle* band, originally called Weltaufstandsplan, inspired by Kraftwerk and not unlike the Residents—except in German. Formed by Kurt Dahlke from Deutsche Amerikanische Freundschaft with Frank Fenstermacher and Moritz Reichelt, they were active between 1979 and 1992, their first album *Geri Reig* (1980), released on their own label Ata Tak, being perhaps their best. Described thus by Terry Rompers of *Trouser Press*: 'Toylike instrumental sounds, tape cut-ups, sing-song vocals, TV theme music and Spike Jones sound effects to create a diverting excursion into the weird and wonderful. Must be heard to be believed.' Der Plan was reformed by Moritz in 2003 with Künstler Treu and JJ Jones.

A MAN, A PLAN, A CANAL—PANAMA!

First published in the 13 November 1948 issue of London's *Notes & Queries*, this tribute to President and Panama Canal champion Theodore Roosevelt (1858–1919) remains perhaps the most famous of all palindromes. It was the work of Leigh Mercer (1893–1977), among his many contributions to the world's drome stock ('Straw? No, too stupid a fad. I put soot on warts'; 'Sums are not set as a test on Erasmus'). The excesses of Daniel Ortega and the American invasion of 1989 inspired several revisions, including 'A man appals: I slap Panama' and 'A man, a pain, a mania—Panama'. In *I Love Me, Vol. I: S. Wordrow's Palindrome Encyclopedia* (1996), Michael Donner lists another recent elongation: 'A man, a plan, a cat, a ham, a yak, a yam, a hat, a canal: Panama.'

MARSHALL PLAN

'It is logical that the United States should do whatever it is able to do to assist in the return of normal economic health in the world without which there can be no political stability and no assured peace. Our policy is directed not against any country but against hunger, poverty, desperation and chaos.' Thus General George Catlett Marshall (1880–1959), US secretary of state, in a commencement address at Harvard on 5 June 1947 which foreshadowed American aid for postwar Europe. When the proposal was welcomed by the foreign ministers of

Great Britain and France, the details were agreed at the Paris Conference on European Economic Co-operation from 12 July. Under the Economic Co-operation Act the US provided $US12 billion in economic aid to Europe over three years; members of the Eastern Bloc were invited to participate but declined. The Marshall Plan stands in acute contrast to the …

MORGENTHAU PLAN

When the Allies were anguishing about the best method of neutralising German influence in postwar Europe after D-Day, the most draconian proposal was devised by treasury secretrary Henry Morgenthau Jnr (1891–1967) and assistant secretary Harry Dexter White (1892–1948). Its vision of a de-industrialised, agrarian Germany was too severe for US secretary of war Henry Stimson and British foreign secretary Anthony Eden, but it is invoked to this day by the extreme right as evidence of a deep-rooted Zionist conspiracy against Aryans involving Morgenthau's friend and neighbour Franklin Roosevelt (1882–1945). Morgenthau, who resigned in July 1945, was first chairman of the United Jewish Appeal. White, who became the first chief of the International Monetary Fund, died of a heart attack before his activities as a Russian agent were revealed.

PLAN 9 FROM OUTER SPACE

So-bad-it's-good 1959 sf film directed by Ed Wood Jnr and featuring Bela Lugosi's last screen appearance—he died after two days of shooting. 'Plan 9' is a program for world conquest conceived by haughty aliens involving the resurrection of corpses from the San Fernando Valley Cemetery. Their objective is to head off a human scheme to develop Solaranite—an explosive that would ignite particles of sunlight. 'Ignite the sunlight here, gentlemen,' declaims the alien ruler, 'and you ignite the sunlight everywhere!' Wood, whose career also involved the transvestite schlockfest *Glen or Glenda* (1953) and the rubber mask revel *Bride of the Monster* (1955), was played by Johnny Depp in Tim Burton's biopic *Ed Wood* (1994); Martin Landau won the Best Supporting Actor Oscar as Lugosi. Plan 9 was also the name adopted by a four-guitar psychedelic garage band from Rhode

Island, best heard on their live album *I've Just Killed a Man I Don't Want to See Any Meat* (1985).

SCHLIEFFEN PLAN

The prophetic German plan for European war drafted by Alfred von Schlieffen (1833-1913), chief of German General Staff, on his retirement in December 1905, in response to the *entente cordiale* agreed the previous year between Britain and France. Envisaging a two-front conflict against the Russians and French supported by the British, Schlieffen urged a holding operation to the east and an offensive to the west, outflanking French fortifications by means of a sweep through Holland, Belgium and Luxembourg—despite Germany's treaty obligation to observe Belgian neutrality. His objective was to rout France before the Russians could fully mobilise, believing that they would be reluctant to enter into conflict if the Germans had already prevailed to the west. Schlieffen refined his plan every Christmas, and it exerted immense influence on German strategic thinking: his successor Helmuth von Moltke (1848–1916) ruled out trespass on Dutch soil, but was untroubled by undertakings to the Belgians. When the Schlieffen Plan was implemented, though, the Belgians responded more robustly and Russians and British more quickly than anticipated; Moltke was sacked, and the antagonists settled into the attrition methods to which they would adhere for most of the next four years.

SCHUMAN PLAN

The brainchild of French planning commissioner Jean Monnet (1888–1979) but championed most successfully by French foreign minister Robert Schuman (1886–1963), a pathfinding scheme of postwar economic co-operation in Europe. On 9 May 1950—whose anniversary is still honoured as Europe Day—Schuman announced that France was inviting Germany to jointly manage their coal and steel industries. The plan became the basis of the European Coal and Steel Community, established two years later, in which Belgium, Italy, Luxembourg and the Netherlands also pooled their coal and steel resources. This group became the basis, six years later, of the European Economic Community.

TEN AGES FROM THE OLD TESTAMENT

Adam 930 ~ Seth 912 ~ Enos 905 ~ Jared 962 ~ Methuselah 969 ~ Noah 950 ~ Shem 600 ~ Mahalaleel 895 ~ Cainan 910 ~ Lamech 777

TEN NIGHTS IN A BARROOM

Written 150 years ago by American novelist Timothy Shay Arthur (1809–1885), *Ten Nights in a Barroom and What I Saw There* was a staple text of the temperance movement for more than half a century. The ten nights in question span ten years in the existence of the Sickle and Sheaf Saloon, licensee Simon Slade, a former miller. The hostelry is glimpsed first in prosperity, but each succeeding cameo involves greater decay. Harvey Green murders his gambling confederate Willy Hammond; Little Mary Morgan is killed when a glass flung by Slade at her drunken father Joe strikes her instead; Slade's mother has a mental breakdown; Slade commits patricide. Cedarvillians finally gather to consider their misfortunes: 'A direful pestilence is in the air—it walketh in darkness, and wasteth at noonday. It is slaying the first-born in our houses, and the cry of anguish is swelling on every gale. Is there no remedy?' But there is: led by Joe Morgan, clean and sober since his daughter's death, a vote is taken closing and liquidating the Sickle and Sheaf, and decreeing prohibition. The novel was adapted four years later for the stage by William Pratt, with the popular song 'Come Home, Father', and twice filmed, in 1909 and 1931.

TEN PEOPLE BORN ON THE TENTH DAY OF THE TENTH MONTH

James Clavell — Alberto Giacometti — Helen Hayes — Paul Kruger — Thelonius Monk — Fritjof Nansen — Harold Pinter — Claude Simon — Giuseppe Verdi — Ben Vereen

TEN METHODS OF CONTRACEPTION AND THEIR EFFECTIVENESS

Method	*Number of pregnancies per 100 women in a year*
Sterilisation	<1
Birth control pill	2.5
IUD	4
Condom with foam	10
Condom without foam	11–14
Diaphragm	18
Sponge	18
Foams/jellies/suppositories	20
Withdrawal	20
Periodic abstinence	24

TEN AFFAIRS

DREYFUS AFFAIR

The son of a Jewish industrialist, Alfred Dreyfus (1859–1935) was in 1894 an army captain in the French War Office suspected of passing secret documents to the German military attaché: a suspicion that quickly turned out to be false but, because of entrenched anti-Semitism in the military, resulted in a prison sentence on Devil's Island that was not commuted even when an investigation led by Colonel Picquart disclosed as the true culprit a Major Esterhazy. A counter-campaign resulted in a retrial at which Dreyfus was nonetheless convicted again—this time by forged documents. President Loubet, however, promptly pardoned him, and the sentence was finally quashed in 1906.

GAIR AFFAIR

In early 1974, Australian prime minister Gough Whitlam approached an old political rival, former leader of the Democratic Labor Party

Vince Gair, about a job as ambassador to Ireland. Senator Gair, an old-fashioned political pugilist, having lost his fight to keep Labor from power, was interested; he could not abide Opposition leader Bill Snedden, whom he had called 'a lightweight who couldn't go two rounds with a revolving door'. The announcement caused a furore, but when Snedden threatened to force an election by blocking Supply in the Senate, Whitlam called his bluff, and a double dissolution election. On 18 May 1974, the government was returned, and Snedden was doomed; he would be replaced by Malcolm Fraser. But not everything worked out: while Gair clung to his appointment, Labor did not obtain the extra Senate vacancy it had sought.

GUINNESS AFFAIR

This 'dishonesty on a massive scale', as it was described by a British High Court judge in August 1990, was perpetrated four years earlier during Guinness's £2.7 billion takeover bid for Distillers. After an investigation that began on the basis of remarks by the convicted Wall Street insider trader Ivan Boesky, Guinness CEO Ernest Saunders, broker Tony Parnes and entrepreneurs Gerald Ronson and Sir Jack Lyons were convicted of artificially propping up the brewer's share price so as to thwart counterbidder Argyll and sentenced to jail terms. Guinness's board was revealed as conspicuously supine. 'It was always easiest to do nothing,' confessed one. 'So I kept my head down.'

HAYMARKET AFFAIR

A bloody moment in the history of American industrial relations, following a series of strikes across the US in favour of an eight-hour day in May 1886. The episode took place at a rally in Chicago's Haymarket organised by an anarchist group to protest the deaths of four people, killed when police opened fire on strikers at the McCormick Harvesting Machine Company. Three hundred protestors were being ordered to disperse by 180 police when a bomb detonated among the latter, of whom one died and seven were mortally wounded. The police opened fire wildly, killing seven and wounding a hundred. A round-up of known radicals followed, and a show trial ensued at which one man was given a long jail term and seven were sentenced to hang: four of these were executed, a fifth hanged himself, and the sixth and seventh had their sentences commuted. The three survivors were pardoned in June 1893.

THE MYSTERIOUS AFFAIR AT STYLES

'A funny little man, a great dandy, but wonderfully clever': thus is introduced for the first time in the fiction of Agatha Christie (1890–1976) the quirky Belgian detective Hercule Poirot. In this 1920 novel, he is called upon by the man who will become his loyal foil, Captain Hastings, to investigate the strychnine poisoning of the wife of Alfred Inglethorp at Styles Court, country seat of the Cavendish family in the Essex village of Styles St Mary. 'This affair must be unravelled from within,' he announces, tapping his forehead: 'These little grey cells. It is "up to them"—as you say over here.'

THE NASTY AFFAIR AT THE BURAMI OASIS

First show of the seventh series of 'The Goon Show', written by Spike Milligan and Larry Stephens, produced by Peter Eton. The forces of Sheik Rattle and Roll are attacking a British garrison by night in order to sap their energies for a forthcoming football match against an Arab team. Gunboat HMS *Thespas*, 42,000 tons, is broken up into four inch squares, packed into crates cunningly marked "date fertilizer, this way up", and dispatched to the trouble spot under the command of Admiral Neddie Seagoon. First aired 4 October 1956.

POULSON AFFAIR

John Poulson, a crooked architect, and George Pottinger, a corrupt civil servant, were sentenced in 1974 to five years jail for bribing politicians on both sides in local government during the building of a winter sports centre in Aviemore, Scotland. T. Dan Smith, leader of the nearby Newcastle City Council, was also imprisoned for six months, and home secretary Reginald Maudling, formerly chairman of two Poulson companies, was compelled to resign, complaining immortally: 'All I wanted was a little pot of money for my retirement.'

PROFUMO AFFAIR

Prostitute Christine Keeler became the best known woman in Britain in June 1963 when it emerged that she had been conducting independent professional relationships with John Profumo, secretary of state for war in the Macmillan government, and Yevgeny Ivanov, Russian naval attaché in London. Profumo, having first denied the rumours, was forced to resign his post; the story emerged that they had met while Keeler was swimming naked at Lord Astor's mansion Cliveden, and introduced by 'society osteopath' Stephen Ward. Keeler's flatmate Mandy Rice-Davies was revealed to be the mistress of infamous slum landlord Peter Rachman. Tried for living off immoral earnings, Ward committed suicide; Keeler was jailed for perjury in another case; the official report on the affair by Lord Denning concluded that security had not been compromised, but criticised the government's tardiness in responding.

SECRET AFFAIR

Mod revivalists inspired by the Jam who released three albums between 1979 and 1982 to steadily diminishing commercial and critical interest. Recalled if at all for their anthemic first single 'Time for Action', but time swiftly passed them by; drummer Seb Shelton was the first member to leave, joining Dexy's Midnight Runners in 1980. Their best recording is the posthumously released *Live at the Bridge* (1997).

THE THOMAS CROWN AFFAIR

Story of a millionaire playboy with a fetish for theft who is pitted against an alluring insurance investigator, filmed twice, in 1968 by Norman Jewison (*The Thrill of It All, Other People's Money*) with Steve McQueen and Faye Dunaway, and in 1999 by John McTiernan (*The Hunt for Red October, Last Action Hero*) with Pierce Brosnan and Rene Russo. The original featured the Oscar-winning song 'The Windmills of Your Mind' by Michael Legrand, and Alan and Marilyn Bergman.

TEN EXPRESSIONS IN LEGAL LATIN

Accusare nemo se debet.
No one is bound to incriminate himself.

Contemporanea exposito est optima et fortissima in lege.
Contemporary exposition is the best and strongest in law.
(The injunction to construe a document in the likely light of its sense at the time of its composition.)

Domus sua cuique est tutissimum refugium.
To each person, his home is the safest refuge.

Ignorantia legis neminem excusat.
Ignorance of the law excuses no one.

Interest reipublicae ut sit finis litum.
It is in the interest of the state that there should be an end to litigation.
(Said in the case of protracted litigation that is not progressing.)

Lex prospicit las.
The law looks forward not back.
(The principle of non-retrospectivity.)

Nemo judex in causa sua.
Nobody should judge their own case.
(The injunction against conflicted interests.)

Res ipsa loquitur.
The thing speaks for itself.

Suspedatur per collum.
Let him be hanged by the neck.

Vigilantibus non dormientibus subveniunt iura.
Law serves the vigilant, not the sleepy.
(The need for plaintiffs to litigate expeditiously.)

TEN MOMENTS IN MILITARY HUBRIS

'We march straight on; we march to victory.'
King Harold rejecting the offer of negotiation before the Battle of Hastings, 1066.

'I am going to fight for my crown and my dignity.'
King Charles I before the Battle of Edgehill, 1642.

'The English never lose ground.'
General John Burgoyne before the Battle of Saratoga, American War of Independence, 1777.

'They couldn't hit an elephant at this distance.'
General John Sedgwick, last words, Spotsylvania Courthouse, Virginia, American Civil War, 1864.

'If they attack us, so much the better; we shall be able, no doubt, to fling them into the Meuse.'
Marshal Maurice McMahon, order to General Lebrun before the French defeat at the Battle of Sedan, Franco-Prussian War, 1870.

'Hurrah, boys, we've got them!'
General George Custer to his troops as they began the Battle of Little Big Horn, 1876.

'Khartoum is all right. Could hold out for years.'
General Gordon's last message to Wolseley's relief force, shortly before being overwhelmed by the Mahdi's army, 1884.

'Smash in the door and the whole rotten structure will come down.'
Adolf Hitler at the launch of Operation Barbarossa, the German invasion of Russia, 1941.

'We're going to wipe the floor with the British.'
General George Stumme in his diary before the Battle of El Alamein, 1942.

'Have no fear for ultimate victory. It is certain that your sacrifices will be rewarded. That is as true as it is true that God is just and Italy is immortal.'
Benito Mussolini in Rome after the Allied invasion of Italy, 1943.

INTERSTATE 10

Interstate 10, one of the longest roads in the continental United States, runs 2460 miles (3936 km) across the south of the country from Santa Monica, California to Jacksonville, Florida, passing en route through Los Angeles (California), Phoenix, Tucson (Arizona), Las Cruces (New Mexico), El Paso, San Antonio, Houston (Texas), Lafayette, Baton Rouge, New Orleans (Louisiana), Mobile (Alabama), Pensacola and Tallahassee (Florida).

TEN NOTABLE MODERN CANADIANS

Bryan Adams — Margaret Atwood — Conrad Black — Wayne Gretsky — Leslie Neilson — John Ralston Saul — Carol Shields — Donald Sutherland — Shania Twain — Galen Weston

FOUNDATION DATES OF TEN AUSTRALIAN ORGANISATIONS

Alcoholics Anonymous	1945
Apex	1931[1]
Industrial Design Council of Australia	1958
Junior Farmers Club	1928[2]
Legacy	1922[3]
National Trust of Australia	1945
Royal Australasian College of Surgeons	1928
Smith Family	1922
Standards Association of Australia	1929
Rotary	1921[4]

[1] First branch in Geelong [2] First branch in Glen Innes, New South Wales
[3] First branch in Hobart [4] First branch in Melbourne

WEBER'S TEN PRECONDITIONS OF OPTIMUM BUREAUCRACY

In his posthumously published *The Theory of Social and Economic Organisations* (1924), sociologist Max Weber (1864–1920) distinguished between three kinds of legitimate authority: rational (typically bureaucratic), traditional (typically hereditary) and charismatic (typically entrepreneurial). The first he thought the most robust, being vested in the office of a person rather than the individual: 'Precision, speed, unambiguity, knowledge of files, continuity, discretion, unity, strict subordination, reduction of friction and of material and personal costs—these are raised to the optimum point in the strictly bureaucratic administration.' He specified ten criteria observed by officials in the purest type of bureaucratic structure:

1. They are personally free, subject only to authority in respect of their impersonal official obligations.
2. They are organised in a clearly defined hierarchy of offices.
3. Each office has a clearly defined sphere of competence in the legal sense.
4. The office is filled by a free, contractual relationship. Thus, in principle, there is free selection.
5. Candidates are selected on the basis of technical qualifications, and appointed not elected.
6. They are remunerated by fixed salaries in money, graded primarily according to their rank in the hierarchy.
7. The office is treated as the sole, or least the primary, occupation of the incumbent.
8. It constitutes a career, with promotion dependent on the judgment of superiors.
9. The official is completely separate from the ownership of the means of the administration.
10. The official is subject to strict and systematic discipline and control.

Astral Crown

Associated with aviators, aviation institutions and distinguished members of the Royal Air Force.

Burghal Coronet

A version of the Mural Crown (*qv*) used by Scottish counties before the reorganisation of local government in 1974.

Crown Vallary

Associated with law and order, particularly police authorities (for the Latin *vallare*, to fortify).

Ducal Coronet

Four strawberry leaves on a chased rim, used on crowned animals in coats of heraldic compositions unless another crown is specified.

Eastern Crown

Associated with distinguished service in the Near or Far East.

Former Scottish Counties

Replaced Burghal coronet.

Saxon Crown

Denoting Saxon associations.

Mural Crown

Associated with the heraldry of distinguished soldiers where such a crown is usually an augmentation.

Naval Crown

Associated with distinguished sailors, and local authorities that have a maritime tradition.

Palisado Crown

Associated with towns that have a Roman connection, or constructed within old fortifications, symbolised by the crown's defensive palisade.

TEN KINDS OF MEDICINE

MEDICINE	WHAT IT TREATS
Analgesic	Pain
Antibiotic	Bacterial infection
Anticoagulant	Clotting
Antifungal	Fungal infection
Antihistamine	Allergies
Antipyretic	Fever
Antitussive	Coughing
Expectorant	Respiratory blockage
Laxative	Constipation
Sedative	Anxiety

THE COUNCIL OF TEN

A secret, often despotic, constitutional tribunal in the world's longest-lasting republic, Venice, formed in 1310 after the Doge Gradenigo foiled the conspiracy of Bajamonte Tiepolo and Mario Querini to restore democracy. Originally provisional, it became permanent during the reign of Francesco Dandolo in 1335, dealing with all significant political, criminal, religious and moral offences. Elections of the Decemvirs, who were appointed for one year and paid nothing, were the responsibility of the Grand Council, a body of between 500 and 2000 from the public's mercantile classes. The Ten consolidated its power in 1355 when it thwarted a plot by the Doge Marino Falieri to make himself despot of Venice, and executed him in the courtyard of the Ducal Palace: the Doge was subsequently reduced to a ceremonial status. After 1539, with the reign of Pietro Lando, three members served as inquisitors of state, maintaining order by means of a secret police, and information received from the *Boccadi Leone* (lion-headed boxes where Venetians could denounce one another); the Ten would then hand down an irrevocable verdict. The Ten was not usurped until Napoleon's war on Austria spilled onto the peninsula: with the Peace of Champoformio in August 1797 that delivered Venice to Austria, the Grand Council was compelled to vote for its own abolition and the Doge Ludovico Manin abdicated.

LITERAL TRANSLATIONS OF TEN PASTAS

Cannelloni little tubes
Farfalle butterflies
Fettucine little slices
Fusilli little spindles
Linguine little tongues
Orecchiette little ears
Penne quill pens
Ravioli little turnips
Spaghetti little strings
Tortellini little tarts

TEN CRICKETERS WHO COULD HARDLY HAVE PLAYED A DIFFERENT GAME

Frank Bale (Leicestershire, 1920–28)
Spencer Block (Surrey, 1928–33)
Arthur Grass (South America, 1932)
Halford Hooker (New South Wales, 1924–32)
Henry Pickett (Essex, 1894–97)
Reginald Scorer (Warwickshire, 1921–26)
John Seamer (Somerset, 1932–48)
Thomas Shooter (Nottinghamshire, 1881)
Andrew Speed (Warwickshire, 1927–28)
Owen Wait (Surrey, 1950–51)

TEN PIRATES

PIRATE	ALIAS	FIELD OF OPERATIONS
Henry Mainwaring (1587–1653)	The Captain	Caribbean
Successful Jacobean pirate, empowered by crown to 'savage Spanish ships', later knighted and promoted to vice-admiral.		
Sam Bellamy (1688–1717)	Black Sam	East coast of North Ameri
Took to piracy in order to provide 'diamonds and jewels' for his fifteen-year-old fiancée.		
John Avery (1653–1696)	Long Ben	Spain, Africa, Madgascar
Subject of play *The Successful Pyrate* by Charles Johnson and novel *Life, Adventures and Pyracies of the Famous Captain Singleton* by Daniel Defo		
William Kidd (1655–1701)	Captain Kidd	Malabar coast of India
Originally commissioned to hunt pirates, his disposition changed after a crew revolt. Undone when the treasure-laden *Quedagh Merchant* he captured proved to belong to the English East India Company. The rope at his execution broke twice. His treasure is the fruit of William Legrand's cryptography in Edgar Allan Poe's 'The Gold Bug' (1843).		
Bartholomew Roberts (1682–1722)	Black Bart	West Indies West Africa
Abstainer and sabbatarian who disapproved of gambling but originated the expression: 'A merry life and a short one shall be my motto.'		

... AND THE FATES THAT AWAITED THEM

FLAGSHIP	FATE
Resistance	Pardoned, allowed to keep booty in 1616. Spent retirement writing about piracy and proposing means of its suppression.
Whydah	Drowned in wreck of *Whydah* off Cape Cod. Of the eight survirors, six were hanged for piracy.
Charles II	Settled at Bideford, Devon, under an assumed name. Cheated of most of his fortune by unscrupulous merchants, he died a pauper.
Adventure Galley	Arrested in New York, hanged in London. The rope at his execution broke twice. His body, dipped in tar and hung by chains on the banks of the Thames, was a symbol of the authorities' resolve to stamp out piracy.
Royal Fortune *Royal Rover*	Ambushed by the British warship *Swallow,* killed by grapeshot off the Guinea coast of Africa.

PIRATE	ALIAS	FIELD OF OPERATIONS
Henry Morgan (1635–1688)	The Sword of England	West Indies

Responsible for the sack of Panama, 1670, but successfully sued William Crooke, publishers of Esquemelig's *History of the Bucaniers of America*, for exaggerating his cruelty.

Thomas Tew (?–1695)	The Robin Hood of the Seas	Red Sea

One-time privateer, turned to piracy to keep the loyalty of a restive crew; plundered Arabian and Indian trade using the 'Libertatia' commune in Madagascar as base.

Edward Teach (?–1718)	Blackbeard	West Indies

Captured more than forty ships in a brief and vicious career; returned to piracy after a pardon and offer of amnesty.

Stede Bonnet (?–1718)	Major Stede, Captain Thomas	Caribbean

Former Barbados sugar plantation owner, turned to piracy because of 'some discomforts he found in married state'.

Howell Davis (?–1719)	The Cavalier Prince of the Pyrates	West Indies, Africa

One of only three real pirates mentioned in *Treasure Island*; 'a most generous humane person' according to contemporary William Snelgrave.

Bartholomew Roberts' flag

FLAGSHIP	FATE
Satisfaction *Oxford*	Captured, imprisoned, tried but pardoned by Charles II; became Jamaica's deputy governor.
Amity	Wounded by cannonfire from the *Fateh Mohamed* and bled to death. Widely mourned and much imitated.
Queen Anne's Revenge	Ambushed by pirate hunters Maynard and Hyde at Ocracoke Inlet; he was decapitated by a highlander's broadsword.
Revenge	Captured by Colonel William Rhett of the *Henry* at Cape Fear River. Bonnet was placed on trial at Charleston, North Carolina, convicted of piracy and hanged.
Royal James	Killed in ambush by the governor of Prince's Island. He was shot five times then had his throat cut.

Stede Bonnet's flag

TEN TEN-STRINGED MUSICAL INSTRUMENTS

adungu . . . . harp of the Alur people from Uganda.
boulou . . . . West African antecedent of the banjo, thought to have been brought to the United States by Negro slaves.
bägänna. . . . . . large Middle Eastern lyre consisting of skin-covered sound box on trapezoidal wooden frame. King David is said to have played it to relieve the insomnia of his stepfather Saul.
charango. . . . . small Andean lute.
cuatro . . . . violin-shaped Puerto Rican instrument played with pick.
kirkincho . . . . charango whose back is carved in the traditional fashion from an armadillo shell.
ngombi . . . . . . Congolese harp, strings stretched between a wooden sound-box and arched branch of wood fitted with small tuning pegs.
pencilina . . . . . . custom-built combination of the hammer dulcima, slide guitar and fretless bass, struck with sticks, plucked and bowed. Designed by Bradford Reed of King Missile III ('Detachable Penis', 'Jesus Was Way Cool'). 'When he's playing the pencilina, the word to describe him is intense.' Colin Moynihan, *New York.*
qin . . . . Chinese zither dating from Tang dynasty. More recent versions feature seven strings.
sarod. . . . . . small sitar with two resonating chambers. Also features fifteen sympathetic strings. The main strings are plucked with coconut shell.

TEN CHAMPAGNE BOTTLE SIZES

Split = (1/4 bottle)
Pint = (1/2 bottle)
Bottle (0.75l, 26fl oz)
Magnum (1.5l, 2 bottles)
Jereboam (3l, 4 bottles)
Rehoboam (4.5l, 6 bottles)
Methuselah (6l, 8 bottles)
Salmanzar (9l, 12 bottles)
Balthazar (12l, 16 bottles)
Nebuchadnezzar (15l, 20 bottles)

TEN EXPRESSIONS FROM CASINO ENGLISH

Blanket roll
In craps, a controlled throw of the dice by an expert hustler seeking a particular number.

Carpet joint
Plush casino attached to a hotel. The opposite of a sawdust joint.

Casedown player
In blackjack, a player capable of keeping mental track of all the cards dealt, thus computing the changing odds. Usually seeks to play to the dealer's right, thus becoming the last to play his hand.

Chemin de fer
A variation of baccarat in which the banker plays against only one opposing hand and must follow certain prescribed rules.

Juice joint
Gambling establishment where dice rolls and roulette wheels are manipulated by house.

Ladderman
Casino employee in an elevated position who watches games of craps and baccarat for signs of cheating.

Las Vegas total
The holistic casino experience: gambling, entertainment, women.

Let it ride
To combine original bet with all winnings and wager them again.

Natural
In baccarat, an eight (La Petite) or nine (La Grande) in the first two cards which wins immediately unless matched or beaten.

Tough money
The money a gambler sets aside for daily essentials: rent, food, etc. It is a law, more often honoured in the breach, that a gambler should not bet with tough money.

TEN RIGHTS OF MAN

In December 1948, the United Nations General Assembly adopted the Universal Declaration of the Rights of Man: the minimum socio-legal entitlements of each human individual. The thirty articles of the charter, of which these are the first ten, were passed without dissent:

ARTICLE 1: All human beings are born free and equal in dignity and rights. They are endowed with reason and conscience and should act toward one another in a spirit of brotherhood.

ARTICLE 2: Everyone is entitled to all rights and freedoms set forth in this declaration, without distinction of any kind, such as race, colour, sex, language, religion, political or other opinion, national or social origin, property, birth or other status.

ARTICLE 3: Everyone has the right to life, liberty and the security of the person.

ARTICLE 4: No one shall be held in slavery or servitude; slavery and the slave trade shall be prohibited in all their forms.

ARTICLE 5: No one shall be subjected to torture or to cruel inhuman or degrading treatment or punishment.

ARTICLE 6: Everyone has the right of recognition everywhere as a person before the law.

ARTICLE 7: All are equal before the law and are entitled without any discrimination to equal protection before the law. All are entitled to equal protection against any discrimination in violation of this declaration and against any incitement to such discrimination.

ARTICLE 8: Everyone has the right to an effective remedy by the competent national tribunals for acts violating the fundamental rights granted to him by the constitution or the law.

ARTICLE 9: No one shall be subjected to arbitrary arrest, detention or exile.

ARTICLE 10: Everyone is entitled in full equality to a fair and public hearing by an independent and impartial tribunal in the determination of his rights and obligations and of any criminal charge against him.

HEIGHTS OF TEN SILENT FILM ACTRESSES

4'9"(144.78cm)............................. Daphne Pollard
4'10"(147.32cm)........... Florence Turner, Francine Larrimore
4'11"(149.86cm)................................. Barbara Kent
5'(152.4cm)..................................... Mary Pickford
5'1"(154.65cm)............................. Norma Shearer
5'2"(157.5cm) .... Gloria Swanson
5'3"(160cm)...................... Fay Wray, Molly Malone
5'4"(162.5cm) .... Paulette Goddard

TEN MAYAN AND AZTEC DEITIES

DEITY	MAYAN	AZTEC
Supreme God	Hunab Ku, Itzamna	Ometeotl
Moon Goddess	Ixchel	Xochiquetzal
Sun God	Kinich Ahau	Tonatiuh
Fertility Goddess	Akhushtal	Coatlicue
Death God	Ah Puch	Mictlantecuhtli

COUNTRIES CROSSED BY THE TENTH DEGREE OF LONGITUDE

WEST: Ireland, Morocco, Western Sahara, Mauritania, Mali, Guinea, Liberia.

EAST: Norway, Denmark, Germany, Austria, Switzerland, Italy, Tunisia, Libya, Algeria, Niger, Nigeria, Cameroon, Equatorial Guinea, Gabon.

TEN SHERLOCK HOLMES PARODIES

DETECTIVE	SIDEKICK	CREATOR	MOST SIGNIFICANT WORK
Sherslav Golmsky	Dr Ivan Vatslov	John Boardman	'The Adventure of the Sinister American' (1959)
Herlock Sholmes	Dr Jotson	Peter Todd	*The Complete Casebook of Herlock Sholmes* (1989)
Shylar Homes	Dr Whatley	Stephen Williams	*The Adventures of Shylar Homes* (1966)
Sherlaw Kombs	Dr Whatson	Luke Sharp (Robert Barr)	'The Great Pegram Mystery' (1892)
Picklock Holes	Dr Potson	Cunnin Toil (R. C. Lehmann)	*The Adventures of Picklock Holes* (1975)
Shirley Holmes	Joan Watson	Frederick Kummer/ Basil Mitchell	'The Adventure of the Queen Bee' (1933)
Shrock Holmes	Dr Harcourt	Bradley Kjell	'The Adventure of the Psychodelic Sleuth' (1968)
Shirley Holmquist	Aunt Wilma	Janet Martin	*Shirley Holmquist and Aunt Wilma: Whodunnit?* (1989)
Schlock Homes	Dr J. Watney	Robert Fish	*The Incredible Schlock Holmes* (1966)
Sheerback Tones	Dr Bopson	Jerry Williamson	'The Adventure of the Bugged Bird' (1960)

SHAKESPEARE'S TENTH SONNET

For shame deny that thou bear'st love to any,
Who for thy self art so unprovident.
Grant, if thou wilt, thou art beloved of many,
But that thou none lov'st is most evident:
For thou art so possessed with murderous hate,
That 'gainst thy self thou stick'st not to conspire,
Seeking that beauteous roof to ruinate
Which to repair should be thy chief desire.
O! change thy thought, that I may change my mind:
Shall hate be fairer lodged than gentle love?
Be, as thy presence is, gracious and kind,
Or to thyself at least kind-hearted prove:
Make thee another self for love of me,
That beauty still may live in thine or thee.

TEN 'TEN' PLACENAMES

Ten Boer — The Netherlands

Ten Degree Channel — Andaman Islands

Ten Hills — Baltimore, USA

Tenerife — Canary Islands

Ten Mile Lake — Newfoundland, Canada

Ten Mile River — New York, USA

Ten Post — The Netherlands

Ten Sleep — Wyoming, USA

Ten Thousand Island — Florida, USA

Valley of Ten Thousand Smokes — Katmai National Park, Alaska, USA

THE DEVELOPMENT OF IN-FLIGHT SERVICE IN TEN PARAGRAPHS

1. The first in-flight meals were offered, from 11 October 1919, by Handley Page Transport on their London to Paris route. Passengers were offered lunch baskets of sandwiches and fruit at 3*s* each. The journey at the time took two hours at about 160kmh, with pilots beginning their journey from Cricklewood Aerodrome by following the number 16 bus route to Marble Arch, then a railway to the coast. Passengers could assess their progress with a ceiling map from British Petroleum, which provided Handley Page with its aviation spirit.

2. The first in-flight refreshment offered on the Queensland and Northern Territory Aerial Service was to its second passenger, Miss Ivy McLain, in November 1922. She was served tea from a thermos at 5000 feet, between Cloncurry and Charleville. Not until 1929, however, did Qantas install its first in-flight toilet aboard its DH61.

3. In the 1920s, Daimler Airways introduced the first dedicated in-flight service personnel, a group of cabin boys. Stewards served on the Argosy Silver Wing Service between London to Paris from May 1927. At the time, though, because flights were relatively short, most meals could still be served on the ground. Eastern Airlines' pioneering service from New York to Miami—promoted with the famous radio jingle 'From frost to flowers in fourteen hours'—stopped in Philadelphia, Baltimore, Washington, Richmond (where lunch was served), Raleigh, Florence, Charleston, Savannah, Jacksonville (where dinner was served) and Daytona Beach. Qantas's first Brisbane to London flight involved forty-two landings and five planes.

4. The first stewardesses were hired in May 1930 by United Airlines (then Boeing Air Transport). All eight were registered nurses. United's first instinct had been to hire men, but applicant Ellen Church pointed out to her interviewer Steve Simson: 'Don't you think it would be better psychology to have women in the air? How is a man going to say that he's afraid to fly when a woman is working on the plane.' Simson wrote to his superior: 'You know nurses as well as I do,

and you know that they are not given to flightiness.' They were all required to be younger than twenty-five, lighter than 52kg, and shorter than 1.62m tall. American Airlines followed suit in 1933, TWA in 1935. The first stewardess in Europe was Nelly Deiner of Swissair. Lufthansa's stewardesses, hired soon after, were required to perform secretarial duties for passengers.

5. The first American Association of Flight Attendants handbook contains the following advice: 'Remember at all times to maintain the respectful reserve of a well-trained servant. A ready smile is essential. Wind the altimeters in the cabin, sweep out the plane and dust the windowsills, swat flies in the cabin and warn passengers against throwing lighted cigar butts out of the windows. Passengers who wish to remove their shoes should be assisted and the shoes cleaned by the hostess before returning them. A final warning—keep a close eye on passengers going to the washroom.' This was easier said than done. Conditions in unpressurised airliners, acutely vulnerable to weather and turbulence, could be extremely trying. In his memoir *Fate Is the Hunter* (1986), pilot Ernest Gann described airline travel in the 1930s from the perspective of aircrew as an intense olefactory experience: 'The airplanes smell of hot oil and simmering aluminum, disinfectant, faeces, leather and puke. The stewardesses, short-tempered and reeking of vomit, come forward as often as they can for what is a breath of comparatively fresh air.'

6. The first airline to encourage passengers to sleep on board was American, which in 1934 turned its Curtiss Condor into a kind of flying Pullman car. It was also the first to make a serious attempt at reliable baggage handling when its president called together all managers for a national conference and all lost their luggage en route.

7. The first Australian hostesses were Rita Gruebner and Blanche Due, two young ladies who answered a newspaper advertisement placed by Holyman Airways in 1936. Dressed in ersatz uniforms from Collins Street clothing boutiques embossed with a Holyman badge, they first dispensed tea and coffee from thermoses on board the airline's DH86s. To Gruebner and Due is owed the fact that beverages are no longer served in wax-coated cups: they noticed that the wax

melted and stuck to passengers' lips. Qantas employed stewards from 1939, although not stewardesses until 1947; they were then hand-picked by Lady Fysh, wife of the chairman Sir Hudson. The first black stewardess in the US, Ruth Carol Taylor of Mohawk Airways, was not hired until 1958.

8. United Airlines was the first airline to conceive of using a tray for passengers, in 1937. At first this was metal, which had aerodynamic implications. In Reg Adkins' memoir of domestic aviation in Western Australia, *I Flew for MMA* (1996), Joy Fawcett recounted: 'Dinner was cold ham and salad and fruit. There were only sixteen trays because the weight factor came in the payload of the DC-3, so you would be waiting for number one to finish so you could hand number seventeen his dinner while you were serving the coffee. So by the time you landed at Albany, the people in the front two rows usually got an apple and an orange thrown at them because one person on their own didn't have time to serve them.'

9. Drinking has been associated with flying since its earliest days, given that passengers sometimes needed to be fortified to have the courage to go aloft. One famous tipple was the Irish coffee—strong coffee and thick cream laced with Irish whiskey with which employees at Ireland's Foynes flying boat terminus revived passengers during the 1940s. One of the last airlines to introduce liquor was Delta, from the American Bible belt, which favoured more genteel touches, like corsages for women and cigars for men. They finally came into line in 1958, despite religious protests.

10. In-flight staff were the subject of a film before they showed one. Jane Wyman, who trained with American Airlines before taking the role, played the role of a stewardess in *Three Guys Named Mike* (1951). She was described as 'enthusiastic to the point of nausea'. Although films were screened on airliners as early as 1929, they did not become convention until the development of a lightweight 16mm film projector thirty years later. The first feature screened in-flight was by TWA: *By Love Possessed* (1961) starring Lana Turner and Efrem Zimbalist Jnr.

TEN LITTLE INDIANS

Set on Indian Island off the Devon coast and based on her novel *And Then There Were None* (1939), Agatha Christie's legendary play was produced as *Ten Little Indians* in the US (1944) and *Ten Little Niggers* (1945) elsewhere. Ten people—eight individuals and a couple in domestic service—have been lured to a lonely guesthouse with varying false explanations. As they mingle, a recorded voice accuses them of 'murders' of different natures, as follows, for which he threatens they will be 'tried':

Edward Armstrong . . surgeon, killed patient while operating drunk.

William Blore . . . . gave evidence that sent bank robber to jail, where he died.

Emily Brent . . . . dispensed with pregnant servant who then drowned herself.

Vera Claythorne . . . . . governess whose charge drowned in her care.

Capt. Philip Lombard. . . . . caused the deaths of twenty-one men in east Africa.

Gen. John Mackenzie . . . . sent wife's lover, a young officer, on lethal mission.

Anthony Marston. . . . . ran over two children in his car.

Thomas and Ethel Rogers. . . . . allowing their ailing spinster mistress to die.

Sir Lawrence Wargrave . . . judge, sentenced innocent man to hang.

TEN ANIMALS WHERE THE MALE CARES FOR THE YOUNG

arrow poison frogs@ — damselfishes^ — jacanas# — mallee fowl# — marmosets* — mouth-breeding bettas^ — phalaropes# — rheas# — seahorses^ — siamangs*

*Mammal #Bird ^Fish @ Amphibian

TEN SLURS THAT MALIGN THE DUTCH

The phrases 'Dutch courage', 'Dutch auction' and 'Dutch treat' remain in free circulation, but at one time they were part of a liberal use of the prefix 'Dutch' as a pejorative. In *The American Language* (1920), H. L. Mencken traced its use back as far as 1608: with the tide of immigration to the new world, 'Dutch' then became the 'Irish' of its time. Herewith ten examples in use a century ago:

Dutch defence	surrender
Dutch leave	absence without leave
Dutch clock	a bedpan
Dutch reckoning	guesswork
Dutch widow	a prostitute
Dutchman's headache	a hangover
Dutch palate	bad taste
Dutch nightingale	a frog
Dutch act	suicide
Dutch bargain	a bad deal

TEN REMOVALS BY SURGERY

appendicectomy	removal of appendix
cholecystectomy	removal of gall bladder
cholelithotomy	removal of gallstones
cystectomy	removal of bladder
hysterectomy	removal of womb
lobectomy	removal of nerve fibres in neck
lithophrotomy	removal of kidney stone
mastectomy	removal of breast
nephrectomy	removal of kidney
osteotomy	removal of any bone

TEN MOST CORRUPT MODERN HEADS OF GOVERNMENT

In March 2004, London-based NGO Transparency International published a table ranking the ten heads of state who had extorted the greatest amount of money from their countries and peoples.

Head of Government	*Estimate of Embezzled Funds*	*GDP per Capita (2001)*
MOHAMED SUHARTO (Indonesia, 1967–98)	US $15 to 35 billion	US $695
FERDINAND MARCOS (Philippines, 1972–86)	US $5 to 10 billion	US $912
MOBUTU SESE SEKO (Zaire, 1965–97)	US $5 billion	US $99
SANI ABACHA (Nigeria, 1993–98)	US $2 to 5 billion	US $319
SLOBODAN MILOSEVIC (Serbia, 1989–2000)	US $1 billion	n/a
JEAN-CLAUDE DUVALIER (Haiti, 1971–86)	US $300 to 800 million	US $460
ALBERTO FUJIMORI (Peru, 1990–2000)	US $600 million	US $2051
PAVLO LAZARENKO (Ukraine, 1996–97)	US $114 to 200 million	US $766
ARNOLDO ALEMÁN (Nicaragua, 1997–2002)	US $100 million	US $490
JOSEPH ESTRADA (Philippines, 1998–2001)	US $78 to 80 million	US $912

TEN VITAL ELEPHANT STATISTICS

1. An elephant usually lives between fifty and seventy years.
2. An elephant's gestation period is twenty-two months.
3. A newborn elephant usually weighs between 80 and 100kg.
4. It is suckled by its mother for between two and a half and five years, and reaches puberty between the ages of twelve and fifteen.
5. A typical elephant feeds for about eighteen hours a day, consuming about 150kg of vegetation.
6. Elephants can eat more than 200 different kinds of plant, including grasses, leaves, fruit and bark.
7. On hot days, an elephant will drink about 200 litres of water, approximately the contents of the average bathtub.
8. The elephant sleeps only four hours a night.
9. In the wild, an elephant can range up to thirty kilometres in a day.
10. An elephant's trunk contains 40,000 muscles—the human body contains 639 in toto—and can hold up to ten litres of water.

TEN SIGNS USED BY HOBOS

The golden age of the American hobo, a phenomenon of the Civil War and the subsequent economic crisis, lasted from the 1870s until the 1920s, when farm mechanisation eliminated many of the casual agricultural jobs on which itinerants had been able to subsist. Within this period, the 'Knights of the Road' composed a flourishing subculture with the expressed philosophy: 'The hobo does not believe that society owes him a living, but he does believe that society owes him a chance to care for himself.' Part of the creed of mutual assistance was the symbolic language used to communicate useful information to other travellers, usually scratched in chalk or coal. Such as:

Kind woman lives here. Tell a pitiful story.

Rich people live here.

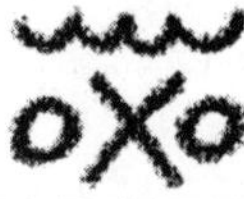

This house is well guarded.

Safe campsite.

Hold your tongue.

Be ready to defend yourself.

Vicious dog lives here.

Religious talk will get you a meal here.

Thieves are about.

Owners here will give to get rid of you.

TEN AUNTS

AUNT AGATHA

In the Jeeves stories of P. G. Wodehouse, stockbroker's wife Agatha Gregson 'has an eye like a man-eating fish' and 'moral suasion down to a fine point', according to her nephew Bertie Wooster: 'My experience is that when Aunt Agatha wants you to do a thing you do it, or else you find yourself wondering why those fellows in the olden days made such a fuss when they had trouble with the Spanish Inquisition.' Inter alia, she wants Bertie to marry Honoria and become secretary to wealthy A. B. Filmer. Bertie also has a kindly aunt, Dahlia Travers.

AUNT AUGUSTA

At his mother's funeral, cloistered and emotionally constipated English bank employee Henry Pulling meets a woman introducing herself as his aunt, Augusta Bertram, who convinces him to take a trip to Brighton. In Graham Greene's *Travels with my Aunt* (1969), this evolves into an exuberant gallivant through Europe and South America, and a gentler inner journey reflecting on Pulling's own life and plight. Augusta was played by Maggie Smith in George Cukor's 1972 screen version.

AUNT CLARA

The accident-prone favourite aunt, played by Marion Lorne, to Samantha, played by Elizabeth Montgomery, in the American witchcraft-in-suburbia sitcom 'Bewitched', which ran for 254 episodes from 1964 to 1972. Notable for her usually calamitous arrivals (e.g. by parachute, down the chimney, through the refrigerator) and her well-meaning but invariably misguided spells. The character was not recast after Lorne's death during the series' fourth season in 1968, shortly after winning an Emmy Award for her role.

AUNT EDNA

The name given by playwright Terence Rattigan (1911–1977) for the kind of person who would most enjoy his works: a 'nice, respectable, middle-class, middle-aged maiden lady, with time on her hands and money to help her pass it, who resides in a West Kensington hotel'.

AUNT FANNY

Remote, irascible valetudinarian married to Uncle Quentin and resident at Kirrin Cottage, whose rather lax standards of adult responsibility permit the Famous Five to indulge their adventurous instincts in the series of books that Enid Blyton (1895–1968) began in 1942.

AUNT JEMIMA

Personification of pancake-making excellence created by Chicago's R. T. Davis Milling Company, based on a real African-American woman, Nancy Green (1834–1923), thus becoming the advertising industry's first 'living trademark'. Her first public appearance at the Chicago exposition of 1893 using Aunt Jemima pancake mixture created a sensation, and she soon became an instantly recognisable face on billboards and products all over the world. The symbol outlived her (she was run down by a car in downtown Chicago) and the company (sold in 1925 to Quaker Oats); her smiling face, somewhat younger, slimmer and smarter, still appears on the product.

AUNTIE MAME

The eponymous heroine of the bestselling 1955 novel by Patrick Dennis (real name Edward Tanner III), subtitled *An Irreverent Escapade*. An adventuress and libertine, with a taste for gin and flair for costume changes, she enjoins her ten-year-old ward: 'Life is a banquet, and most poor sons of bitches are *starving* to death. Live!' Her charge comes to see Mame as 'a froth of whipped cream and champagne and daydreams and Nuit de Noël perfume'. Played by Rosalind Russell in Morton Da Costa's 1958 movie, and by Lucille Ball in 1974 version of the Broadway musical by Jerome Lawrence and Robert E. Lee. John Cleese claimed to have been very disappointed by the latter, believing that he had been going to see a film called *Maim*.

AUNT THEODORA

Miserable spinster Theodora Goodman in Patrick White's 1948 novel *The Aunt's Story*. After a disappointed life in which she has been consoled only by the mutual affection she enjoys with her niece Lou, she is liberated from a life of servitude by the death of her tyrannical mother and sets off to Europe and the US to belatedly experience the world. But she is unable to establish relationships in which she is not cast as an aunt, and descends gradually into madness haunted by questions: 'Why then…is this world which is so tangible in appearance so difficult to hold?'

CHARLEY'S AUNT
Enduringly successful West End farce devised by Brandon Thomas (1856–1914) and first produced in 1892. Oxford fop Babbs Babberleyn helps two of his chums in their wooing by slipping into drag to play a Brazilian matron to act as their chaperone. Played by Charlie Ruggles (1930) and Jack Benny (1941) in two film versions.

THE SOI-DISANT AUNT/THE AUNT-BY-ASSERTION
So described in the short story 'The Lumber Room' (1914) by Saki (1864–1916), a 'woman of few ideas, with immense powers of concentration' and 'one of those people who think that things spoil by use and consign them to dust and damp by way of preserving them' who pays dearly for forbidding the disgraced Nicholas from entering the gooseberry garden.

TEN MURDERS DEFINED

Homicide	person
Mariticide	spouse
Matricide	mother
Parricide	kinsman
Patricide	father
Regicide	king
Sororicide	sister
Suicide	self
Uxoricide	wife
Vaticide	prophet

TEN PREHISTORIC ANIMALS STILL IN EXISTENCE

Peripatus	worm	500 million years old
Coelacanth	fish	400 million years old
Horseshoe crab	crustacean	300 million years old
Turtle	reptile	275 million years old
Tuatara	reptile	200 million years old
Australian lungfish	fish	200 million years old
Stephens Island frog	amphibian	170 million years old
Crocodile	reptile	160 million years old
Platypus	monotreme	150 million years old
Okapi	mammal	30 million years old

TEN US ARMY GROUPS

Unit . . . . two soldiers
Squad . . . . five to ten soldiers (commanded by sergeant)
Platoon . . . . four squads or thirty to fifty soldiers (commanded by lieutenant)
Company . . . . two platoons or 100–200 soldiers (commanded by captain)
Battalion . . . . two to five companies or 500–1000 soldiers (commanded by lieutenant colonel)
Group . . . . two battalions
Brigade . . . . two groups or 2000–4000 soldiers (commanded by colonel)
Division . . . . three brigades or 10,000–17,000 soldiers
Corps . . . . two divisions
Field Army . . . . two corps

SIGHT AND SOUND TOP TENS

Every ten years since 1952, the British Film Institute's *Sight and Sound* magazine has undertaken an extensive poll to determine the best films of all time. The 2002 poll surveyed the opinions of 145 critics. These are the results of it and the first.

1952		2002	
1	*Bicycle Thieves* (De Sica)	1	*Citizen Kane* (Welles)
2	*City Lights* (Chaplin)	2	*Vertigo* (Hitchcock)
2	*The Gold Rush* (Chaplin)	3	*La Règle du Jeu* (Renoir)
4	*Battleship Potemkin* (Eisenstein)	4	*The Godfather* and *The Godfather Part II* (Coppola)
5	*Intolerance* (Griffith)	5	*Tokyo Story* (Ozu)
5	*Louisiana Story* (Flaherty)	6	2001: *A Space Odyssey* (Kubrick)
7	*Greed* (von Stroheim)	7	*Battleship Potemkin* (Eisenstein)
7	*Le Jour se Lève* (Carné)	7	*Sunrise* (Murnau)
7	*The Passion of Joan of Arc* (Dreyer)	9	*8½* (Fellini)
10	*Brief Encounter* (Lean)	10	*Singin' in the Rain* (Kelly, Donen)
10	*Le Million* (Clair)		
10	*La Règle du Jeu* (Renoir)		

TEN PHILOSOPHIES OF LORELEI LEE

Gentlemen Prefer Blondes (1925) by Anita Loos (1893–1981), the 'diary' of diamond-fancying Lorelei Lee first published as a serial in *Harper's Bazaar,* is one of the great comic artifacts of the Jazz Age. It was also classed by George Santayana 'the best book of philosophy written by an American'. Herewith, ten philosophical musings of its heroine.

On Consciousness: 'A gentleman friend and I were dining at the Ritz…and he said that if I took a pencil and paper and put down all my thoughts it would make a book. This almost made me smile as what it would really make would be a whole row of encyclopediacs. I mean, I seem to be thinking practically all of the time.'

On Political Correctness: 'He has sent me a whole complete set of books for my birthday by a gentleman called Mr Conrad. They all seem to be about ocean travel…I mean I do not know why authors cannot say "Negro" instead of "Nigger" as they have their feelings just the same as we have.'

On Language: 'Gerry likes to talk a lot and I always think a lot of talk is depressing and worries your brains with things you never even think of when you are busy.'

On the Transience of Human Affection: 'Kissing your hand may make you feel very good but a diamond bracelet lasts forever.'

On Lateral Thinking: 'I mean I think a diamond tiara is delightful because it is a place I really never thought of wearing diamonds before, and I thought I had almost one of everything until I saw a diamond tiara.'

On Freud: 'Dr Froyde said that all I needed was to cultivate a few inhibitions.'

On Jokes: 'So of course I laughed very very loud and I told Piggie he was wonderful the way he could tell jokes. I mean you can always tell when to laugh because Piggie always laughs first.'

On Anglo-Australian Relations: 'I often remember Papa back in Arkansas, and he often he used to say that his grandpa came from a place in England called Australia…'

On Self-Control: 'Henry said that when he looked at all of those large size diamonds he really felt that they did not have any sentiment, so he was going to give me his class ring from Amherst College instead. So then I looked at him and looked at him, but I am to full of self-controle to say anything at this stage of the game, so I said it was really very sweet of him to be so full of nothing but sentiment.'

On Acting: 'I overheard Dorothy talking to Mr Montrose and she was telling Mr Montrose that she thought I would be great in the movies if he would write me a part that only had three expressions, Joy, Sorrow and Indigestion.'

TEN NIETZSCHEAN MAXIMS

As supplements to his *Human, All Too Human* (1878), Friedrich Nietzsche (1844–1900) published two books of musings, mots and aperçus: *Assorted Opinions and Maxims* (1879) and *The Wanderer and His Shadow* (1880). Here are ten:

1. You will never get the crowd to cry Hosanna until you ride into town on an ass.
2. So long as you are praised think only that you are not yet on your own path but on that of another.
3. That which we do not know or feel precisely while awake…the dream informs us of without any ambiguity.
4. You gave him an opportunity of showing greatness of character and he did not seize it. He will never forgive you for that.
5. Not every end is a goal. The end of a melody is not its goal; but nonetheless, if the melody had not reached its end it would not have reached its goal either.
6. The most dangerous follower is he whose defection would destroy the whole party; that is to say, the best follower.
7. What is the vanity of the vainest man compared with the vanity which the most modest possesses when, in the midst of nature and the world, he feels himself to be a 'man'!
8. We would not let ourselves be burned to death for our opinions; we are not sure enough of them for that. But perhaps for the right to have our opinions and to change them.
9. Only the most acute and active animals are capable of boredom—A theme for a great poet would be God's boredom on the seventh day of creation.
10. What does not kill me makes me stronger.

RADIO 10 CODE

10-1	signal weak	10-18	urgent
10-2	signal good	10-19	(in) contact
10-3	stop transmitting	10-20	location
10-4	OK	10-21	telephone
10-5	relay to	10-22	disregard
10-6	busy	10-23	arrived at scene
10-7	out of service	10-25	report to
10-9	repeat	10-26	estimated time of arrival
10-10	negative	10-27	licence details
10-12	standby	10-29	records check
10-13	existing conditions	10-30	danger/caution
10-14	message/information	10-31	pickup
10-15	message delivered	10-33	urgent assistance
10-16	reply to message		

LOUIS X

A member of France's Capetian dynasty known variously as Louis the Quarrelsome and Louis the Stubborn, Louis X (1289–1316), Count of Champagne, King of the Franks and Navarre, ruled France in an undistinguished fashion for twenty months from November 1314, mostly under the influence of his uncle Charles of Valois, after succeeding his father Philippe IV. He married Marguerite de Bourgogne, who bore him a daughter before her imprisonment on trumped-up charges of adultery, then Hungarian noble Clemence d'Anjou, being succeeded on the throne by their son, unborn at the time of his death.

TEN SLANG TERMS FOR MONEY

Ackers — Boodle — Brass — Gelt — Lucre — Oof — Pelf — Shekels — Spondulics — Tin

TEN PHILANTHROPIC ENTERPRISES OF ANDREW CARNEGIE

In his manifesto *The Gospel of Wealth* (1889), the American tycoon Andrew Carnegie (1835–1919) argued forcefully that the wealthy had a moral obligation to serve as stewards for society: 'No man becomes rich unless he enriches others.' After selling his interests in the steel industry to J. Pierpont Morgan's US Steel in 1901 at the age of sixty-five, he lived up fully to his philosophy, turning an abiding interest in philanthropy into a compulsion. He received between 400 and 500 letters a day from those seeking his indulgence and bestowed on various charitable causes and institutions sums worth about 90 per cent of his aggregate wealth: about $US332 million. These included:

* $25,000 towards the construction of a swimming bath in his native Dumferline, Scotland: his first benefaction, in 1873.
* 2500 free libraries.
* 7689 church organs (after a donation to the Swedenborgian church in Allegheny which his father had attended).
* New York's Carnegie Hall, inaugurated in 1891 with a concert conducted by Tchaikovsky.
* Carnegie Technical Schools, founded in 1900, which from 1912 was the Carnegie Institute of Technology—now part of Carnegie-Mellon University.
* $5 million for the Carnegie Hero Fund Commission, a charity for citizens putting their lives at risk for the sake of others, after the deaths of rescuers at the Hawick coal mine disaster in January 1904.
* $36 million for Pittsburgh's Carnegie Institute, consisting of a museum, library, art collection and music hall.
* Funds for the construction of the artificial lake at Princeton (to allow 'a rowing crew to compete with Harvard').
* Initial capital for the Carnegie Endowment for International Peace, founded in 1910. Its Palace of Peace in the Hague was completed three years later.
* The Central American Court of Justice in Costa Rica, completed in 1910 and destroyed shortly after by an earthquake.

TEN DAYS THAT NEVER HAPPENED

Among other changes, the introduction of the Gregorian calendar by Pope Gregory XIII to replace the old and inaccurate Julian calendar entailed the elimination of ten days, following recommendation of the Council of Trent which he had attended as a representative of his predecessor Paul III: Thursday 4 October 1582 (Julian) was followed immediately by Friday, 15 October (Gregorian). At the same time, Pope Gregory decreed that henceforth the year was to begin on 1 January, instead of 1 March as previously. For further and better particulars see David Ewing Duncan's *The Calendar* (1999).

TEN GOLDEN RULES OF SAFE SWIMMING

1. Swim between the flags.
2. Always swim, windsurf and kitesurf at places patrolled by lifesavers or lifeguards.
3. Read and obey all warning signs.
4. If you get into trouble, do not panic. Raise your arm for help, float and wait for assistance.
5. If you are unsure of surf conditions, ask a lifesaver. If you are still unsure, do not go near the water.
6. Never swim alone. Children should always swim under supervision.
7. Be sun-smart. Use 15+ and 30+ sunscreen, and wear a long-sleeve shirt, hat and sunglasses.
8. Never run and dive into the water, even if you have checked the depth.
9. Do not swim under the influence of alcohol or drugs.
10. Do not swim directly after a meal. Allow at least two hours to pass to avoid the risk of cramps.

Published by Water Safety Victoria

TEN LEFT-HANDERS

Allan Border — George Bush — Bill Clinton — Bob Dylan —
Albert Einstein — Queen Elizabeth II — Bill Gates —
Paul McCartney — Harry Truman — Queen Victoria

TEN FINANCIAL MARKETS COLLOQUIALISMS

Alligator Spread: A position whose spread is so large that it ends up devouring the client's cash.

Bed and Breakfasting: Selling securities on the last day of a tax year and buying them back on the next to crystallise a tax loss.

CAMEL: Mnemonic for the five qualities of banks scrutinised by regulators: Capital adequacy – Asset quality – Management quality – Earnings – Liquidity.

Cocktail Swap: A complicated transaction involving multiple swaps and counterparties.

Dead Cat Bounce: The slight bounce in value enjoyed by a security which has recently fallen a long way, sometimes mistaken for a trend. Based on the theory that a dead cat will bounce if dropped from a tall enough building.

Kerb Trading: Trading outside the official hours of an exchange.

Maginot Spread: The difference in yields between German (*bunds*) and French (*obligations assimilables de Tresor*) government bonds.

Texas Hedge: What looks like a strategy for risk minimisation that turns out to exacerbate the size or volatility of an exposure.

Tombstone: Advertisement in the financial press announcing the completion of a deal, issue or syndication, listing those institutions involved and a précis of the terms.

Triple Witching Hour: In the US, the close of trading on the last Friday of each quarter when stock options, future options and futures contracts expire simultaneously.

DUDLEY SMITH

James Ellroy's *Clandestine* (1982), *LA Confidential* (1990) and *White Jazz* (1992)

Tall, imposing, Irish-born, Los Angeles-bred, detective. A family man with five daughters and a charming personality, he nonetheless harbours a violent, sadistic streak that is loosed on drug addicts, homosexuals, minorities and other 'degenerates'.

HARRIET SMITH

Jane Austen's *Emma* (1816)

Dim-witted, illegitimate teenage protégé of Emma Woodhouse at Mrs Godard's School described as 'short, plump, and fair, with a fine bloom, blue eyes, light hair, regular features, and a look of great sweetness'. On Emma's advice that he is beneath her social station, Harriet initially declines Robert Martin's proposition of marriage.

INNOCENT SMITH

G. K. Chesterton's *Manalive* (1912)

Vibrant eccentric who 'somehow made the giant stride from babyhood to manhood, and missed that crisis in youth when most of us grow old'. He breaks into his own house and has an affair with his wife, among other exploits, in order to feel that his life is truly lived: 'He filled every one with his own half-lunatic life; but it was not expressed in destruction, but rather in a dizzy and toppling construction.'

MARY SMITH

E. M. Delafield's *The Diary of a Provincial Lady* (1930)

Softly spoken diarist who charts the 'goings on' in her shabby-genteel country house in an English village of the 1930s. Married to incurably boring Robert, usually found asleep behind his copy of *The Times*, who is agent to snobbish Lady Boxe. Their two children Vicky and Robin, French governess and cook make up the household.

MRS SMITH

Jane Austen's *Sense and Sensibility* (1811) and *Persuasion* (1818)

Name conferred on two characters: the cousin of charming and penniless John Willoughby in *Sense and Sensibility* and the quondam governess to plucky Anne Elliott in *Persuasion.*

PERRY EDWARD SMITH

Truman Capote's *In Cold Blood* (1966)

Dreamy, detached, disturbing murder partner of Dick Hickock, whose plan to kill Kansas farmer Herbert Clutter and his family is brutally realised. On the run, they start a bizarre road-trip from Kansas City, through Mexico, Miami and Vegas, during which Perry grows increasingly disaffected, but is too fearful to break away, and his capture, conviction and execution are made to seem inevitable.

PURDY SMITH

Henry Handel Richardson's *The Fortunes of Richard Mahony* (1917–1930)

Richard Mahony's best man, a ne'er-do-well shot in the ankle at the Eureka Stockade, left with a permanent limp, and apparently blighted fortunes. His fortunes are revived by dabbling in the sharemarket, which infuriates Mahony: 'To see Purdy, the foolish harum-scarum, the confessed failure, the mean little *commis voyageur*—to see such a one about to pass, surpass him, in means and influence: this was surely one of the bitterest mouthfuls he had ever had to swallow.'

SEPTIMUS WARREN SMITH

Virginia Woolf's *Mrs Dalloway* (1925)

Sensitive soul wracked by his wartime experiences and bent on a course of self-destruction when he walks down the same street as Clarissa Dalloway and stops to look at the same aeroplane overhead. Destined to commit suicide the same day as Clarissa stages a dinner party. Played by Rupert Graves in the 1997 screen adaptation.

VIOLET SMITH

Sir Arthur Conan Doyle's 'The Solitary Cyclist' (1904)

'Tall, graceful and queenly' music teacher daughter of famous conductor, heir to the fortune of her late uncle Ralph, object of the unwanted attentions of Bob Carruthers and Jack Woodley. She enlists Sherlock Holmes in April 1895 to unravel the mystery of 'the solitary cyclist of Charlington' who appears each week on the road she travels.

WINSTON SMITH

George Orwell's *1984* (1949)

Low-level, rat-averse functionary in totalitarian Oceania who, with his paramour Julia, hankers to join the subversive Brotherhood. Betrayed by Inner-Party member O'Brien, he is tortured into renunciation of his beliefs by the Ministry of Love.

TEN COMMONEST ELEMENTS ON LAND AND SEA

	Land		*Sea*
1.	Oxygen	1.	Oxygen
2.	Silicon	2.	Hydrogen
3.	Aluminium	3.	Chlorine
4.	Iron	4.	Sodium
5.	Calcium	5.	Magnesium
6.	Sodium	6.	Sulphur
7.	Potassium	7.	Calcium
8.	Magnesium	8.	Potassium
9.	Titanium	9.	Bromine
10.	Hydrogen	10.	Carbon

TEN NEWSPAPER CLICHES

In *MediaWrite: The Unchanging Cliches of Newspaper English* (1989), Fritz Speigl lists many of the 'stilted, unnatural and outdated forms of English' that are common coin on the pages of newspapers. Here are ten of his acute definitions:

BREAKTHROUGH Any advance, achievement or discovery eg medical or scientific; or the promise of a successful end to negotiations. It might be appropriate for, say, the Channel Tunnel; but 'a major breakthrough in surgery' implies that the surgeon and his assistants shook hands through a hole in the patient. In a letter to *The Times* (15 August 1988) a reader reported finding four 'breakthroughs' in a single issue of the paper and assumed there must be a lot of holes somewhere. Another assumed they might have been caused by all the 'tips of icebergs' he kept reading about. They came from World War I, when breaking through the enemy's lines was something accomplished in a real sense. The word is not even English, merely naturalised, a clumsy wartime translation of the German military term *Durchbruch*, and unknown before that war.

COPYCAT The cat is a proud, independent creature and does not imitate humans.

DEAD MEN They may not be able to tell tales but in newspaper reports they can do all manner of things long after death, eg, 'The dead man spent six weeks living with his sister...' or 'The dead woman was taken shopping in Marks & Spencers shortly before she disappeared...' Didn't the other shoppers *mind*? Also DEAD MAN WAS UNFIT TO DRIVE. Hardly surprising.

'FAMOUS FIVE' CLICHE From a book title by Enid Blyton, which pertains to any news story involving more than one person, usually miscreants. From the 'Bradford Eleven', the 'Cheltenham Ten' and the 'Sharpeville Six', to the 'Shrewsbury Two', at any rate until one was released. Not even the silliest tabloid could then bring itself to refer to the remaining prisoner as the 'Shrewsbury One'. If the press had been present...in Israel 2000 years ago the Apostles would doubtless have been dubbed the 'Gethsemane Twelve'.

LONER Usually a convicted man about whom the reporter was unable to find any information.

MANDARIN High-ranking civil servant...scientists are BOFFINS; university teachers are DONS; mentors or advisers GURUS; bosses SUPREMOS; and experts—often self-appointed—PUNDITS.

PUMPED Emotive and sensationalising term ('The SAS man then pumped six shots into him...'). Shots are fired, not pumped—though there exists a pump-action shotgun, which refers to the way it is loaded, not fired.

PURRFECT! Kneejerk joke for any story involving—but oh, you've *guessed*! How clever of you.

SCRIBE Journalists' mock-deprecatory self-description.

VISIBLY MOVED What people are before WEEPING OPENLY. The invisibly moved are not worth mentioning.

THE SUBMERGED TENTH

The poorest tenth of the population of Victorian England, taking their name from the second chapter of *In Darkest England and the Way Out* (1890) by the religious and social reformer William Booth (1829–1919). 'This Submerged Tenth,' he asked. 'Is it, then, beyond the reach of the nine-tenths in the midst of whom they live, and around whose homes they rot and die?' His proposition, work colonies, became a feature of the approach of the Salvation Army with which, as 'General' Booth, he is generally associated.

TEN COMMON SYMBOLS ON ORIENTEERING MAPS

Cave opening

Cliff

Depression

Earth bank

Logged area

Open land

Pond

Quarry

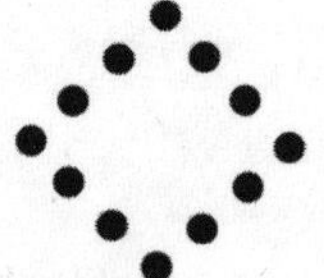

Rough open land

Waterhole

TEN IMPORTANT TWENTIETH-CENTURY TREATIES

BREST-LITOVSK TREATY

3 March 1918

Signed in Brest-Litovsk in Belarus, after four months of negotiation between Russia and the Central Powers of Germany, Austria-Hungary, Bulgaria and Turkey, who 'resolved to live henceforth in peace and amity'. Talks between Leon Trotsky, Germany's Richard von Kühlmann and Austria's Count Ottokar Czernin had almost foundered on several occasions, but the signing of the document abruptly tilted the balance of the Great War by allowing Germany to concentrate its forces on the Western Front.

TREATY OF VERSAILLES

28 June 1919

Signed, on the fifth anniversary of the Sarajevo assassination of Archduke Franz Ferdinand, in the Hall of Mirrors at the Palace of Versailles after six acrimonious months of negotiation in Paris involving Britain's Lloyd George, France's Georges Clemenceau and Woodrow Wilson of the United States. It provided principally for the demobilisation and disarmament of Germany, the division of its foreign possessions, the re-creation of Poland, the dismemberment of the Austro-Hungarian Empire, and the formation of the League of Nations. Composed of fifteen parts, 440 articles and a score of annexes, the most controversial being the Allied demand of reparations.

LOCARNO PACT

16 October 1925

Signed in the Swiss city of Locarno, this was the zenith of the fortunes of the League of Nations: an agreement undergirding the 'territorial status quo' aimed at 'permanent peace' involving the 'plenipotentiaries' of Great Britain, Germany, France, Belgium and Italy, who purported to be 'anxious to satisfy the desire for security and protection which animates the peoples upon whom fell the scourge of war of 1914–1918'.

LONDON NAVAL TREATY

22 April 1930

Signed after the arduous London Naval Conference which sought to prevent initiatives for the re-armament of Germany and Japan by restricting the tonnage of the world's navies. Article 21, however, an 'escalator clause' that allowed signatories to abrogate the treaty if 'materially affected by new construction of any other Power', limited its effectiveness.

THE MUNICH AGREEMENT

29 September 1938

Signed in Munich by Hitler, Mussolini, Britain's Neville Chamberlain and France's Edouard Daladier, this synonym for appeasement, following Germany's annexation of Austria on 12 March 1938, allowed it to add Czechoslovakia to its imperium in return for disavowing further territorial claims in Europe, but bought less than a year of further peace.

THE AXIS TRIPARTITE PACT

27 September 1940

Signed in Berlin by representatives of Germany, Japan and Italy in what it described as 'the eighteenth year of the Fascist era', this document provided for co-operation between the signatories in pursuing their territorial ambitions, specifying that they considered it 'the prerequisite of lasting peace that every nation in the world shall receive the space to which it is entitled'.

THE YALTA TREATY

11 February 1945

Signed covertly by Stalin, Churchill and Roosevelt when Stalin demanded a string of territorial demands in breach of the Atlantic Charter agreed two years earlier, which was not revealed by the State Department until 24 March 1947. It restored to Russia territories lost in the Russo-Japanese war forty years earlier, and consolidated the Russian sphere of influence in the east.

NORTH ATLANTIC TREATY

4 April 1949

Drafted by the foreign ministers of Great Britain, France, Belgium, the Netherlands and Luxembourg, who had invited the US and Canada into a security alliance for mutual defence, and signed in Washington by these nations, along with Norway, Denmark, Iceland, Italy and Portugal. The birth of the North Atlantic Treaty Organisation obliged the signatories to 'refrain in their international relations from the threat or use of force in any manner inconsistent with the purposes of the United Nations', but empowered them to 'maintain and develop their individual and collective capacity to resist armed attack'.

TREATY OF ROME

25 March 1957

Signed by France, Germany, Italy, Belgium, Luxembourg and the Netherlands creating two supranational bodies, the European Economic Community (EEC) and European Atomic Energy Community (EAEC), it prefigured European integration. Both bodies were subsumed by the European Community, precursor to the European Union.

TREATY OF MAASTRICHT

2 February 1992

Signed by the members of the European Community at Maastricht in the Netherlands, what is more formally referred to as the Treaty on European Union brought about the Euro as a common currency and bound the parties to conclude common social and political policies through the European Commission, European Parliament and European Court of Justice. The treaty came into force on 1 November 1993.

TEN DISEASES OF THE LIVER

Budd-Chiari Syndrome — Byler Disease — Caroli Disease — Cirrhosis — Glycogen Storage Disease — Hemochromatosis — Hepatitis (A, B, C, D, E, G) — Galactosemia — Hemangioma — Porphyria

RUPERT MURDOCH AS SEEN BY TEN BIOGRAPHERS

NEIL CHENOWETH
'He is a superb opportunist, and like many opportunists, he is too ordinary to classify. Murdoch is an unprepossessing man, drab to the point of colorlessness, who has built a worldwide empire that has immeasurably changed the way we communicate.'
Virtual Murdoch (2002)

JAMES CRAINER
'Murdoch has talked of having a moral compass to all his activities. However, if there is a morality, it is difficult to find.'
Business the Murdoch Way (1999)

HAROLD EVANS
'Every editor, and many a politician who deals with Murdoch, thinks that they're the one who is going to really change him. They're like a woman who goes out with a womanizer…He has this fatal capacity to instill the confidence in you that you and he have a special, exclusive relationship.'
Good Times, Bad Times (1983)

THOMAS KIERNAN
'His daily mood and outlook were almost childishly affected by every minuscule shift in one or more of his corporations' latest fiscal reports. This psychic condition was not so much a matter of greed or a sense of fiscal responsibility as it was of—well, vindication…So long as his weekly corporate balance sheets reflected vigorous overall profitability, he was able to suppress the underlying guilt and chagrin he felt about his newspaper practices and convince himself that what he was doing was worthwhile.'
Citizen Murdoch (1986)

Michael Leapman
'Chances are that he will continue to live dangerously, bidding for almost anything that is going and buying some of it; hiring, firing, cajoling, telephoning, browbeating employees and politicians alike, living out of a suitcase and flying by the seat of his pants.'
Barefaced Cheek: The Apotheosis of Rupert Murdoch (1983)

George Munster
'Rupert Murdoch turned out to be a person without a hidden self; he is what he does; his actions resolve themselves into a pattern of half a dozen manoeuvres in which he has become highly skilled.'
Rupert Murdoch: A Paper Prince (1987)

Bruce Page
'Murdoch, loudly and more consistently than any other Western publisher, presented himself for thirty years as gripped by an over-mastering preference for freedom...Murdoch's preference for freedom only holds when the cost to himself is zero.'
The Murdoch Archipelago (2003)

Simon Regan
'He reflects in many ways that country's [Australia's] burning desire to prove itself to the rest of the world. He has the deep-rooted inferiority complex which is covered by the customary brashness and nervous cheek of the Australian nature. His action is a kind of cocky, yet somehow self-defensive, show of aggressive brilliance.'
Rupert Murdoch: A Business Biography (1976)

Wendy Goldman Rohm
'Murdoch is a man of shifting tastes and loyalties; he is an iconoclast who traffics in icons.'
The Murdoch Mission (2002)

William Shawcross
'Beyond the empire, he has no interests apart from his family, to whom he is devoted. He finds it virtually impossible to relax. He does

not read books, nor listen to music, nor enjoy museums...He does not sleep well. In his early sixties he is still a man possessed—and lonely.'
Rupert Murdoch: Ringmaster of the Information Circus (1992)

JEROME TUCCILLE
'When I asked him what drives him, he seemed a bit perplexed, as though he didn't quite know what to make of the question. He simply does what he does because he has to; it's in his nature to work and plan and strive and achieve, and I don't believe he's taken a lot of time to analyze what's behind it all.'
Rupert Murdoch (1989)

TEN AMERICANS WHO HAVE DROPPED 'JUNIOR' FROM THEIR NAMES

Kareem Abdul-Jabbar (originally Ferdinand Alcindor Jnr) — Marlon Brando — William Buckley — Jimmy Carter — Jimmy Connors — Bill Cosby — Clint Eastwood — Alexander Haig — Robert Redford — Kurt Vonnegut

ANAGRAMS FOR TEN US PRESIDENTS

George Washington .... I Hog A Regent's Gown
Abraham Lincoln .... A Bill Anchorman
Teddy Roosevelt .... Love to Try Deeds
William Taft .... A Fat Man, I Lilt
Warren G. Harding .... Err? Had Warning
Harry S. Truman .... Tsar Man, Hurry!
Richard Nixon .... Rancor Hid Nix
Ronald Reagan .... A Long Era, Darn!
William Clinton .... An Ill Clown? I'm It
George Bush .... He Bugs Gore

THE TEN FLASHMAN NOVELS

Based on a fictional cache of diaries and letters 'discovered' in a Leicester sales room in 1966, this enduringly popular series by George MacDonald Fraser (b. 1925) tells the imagined life of the bully and rogue who persecutes the hero of *Tom Brown's Schooldays* (1857) by Thomas Hughes (1822–1895). Sir Harry Flashman VC, as he soon becomes, strides through ten novels. Settings change, but Flashman remains impervious to his circumstances, a cowardly, lecherous reprobate throughout all his adventures.

Flashman (1969) . . . . First Anglo-Afghanistan War
Royal Flash (1970) . . . . Schleswig-Holstein
Flash for Freedom (1971). . . . . West Africa, New Orleans
Flashman at the Charge (1973) . . . . Crimean War
Flashman in the Great Game (1975). . . . . Indian Mutiny
Flashman's Lady (1977). . . . . Madagascar, pitted against Queen Ranavalona I
Flashman and the Redskins (1982) . . . . . . The Wild West up to and including Little Big Horn
Flashman and the Dragon (1985). In China, amid the Taiping Revolt
Flashman and the Mountain of Light (1990). . . In the Punjab, on the Northwest Frontier
Flashman and the Angel of the Lord (1994). . As a spy in America just before the Civil War

Also featuring Flashman are *Flashman and the Tiger: Extracts from the Flashman Papers* (1977), a collection of three Flashman tales, and *Black Ajax* (1999), in which Flashman's father, 'Mad Buck', is one of the chief dramatis personae.

THE FIRST TEN PRIME NUMBERS

2, 3, 5, 7, 11, 13, 17, 19, 23, 29

Angola

Barbados

Guatemala

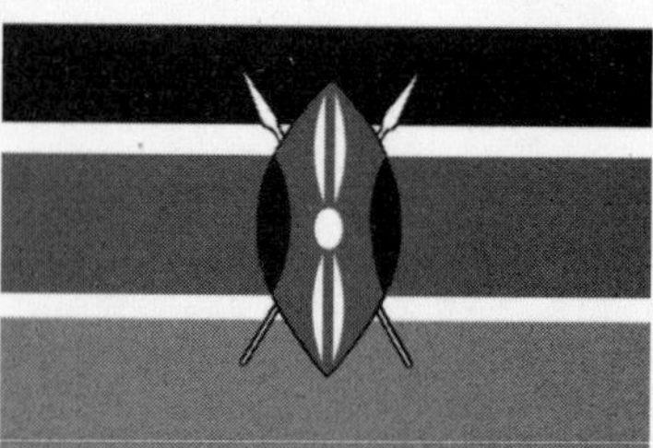

Kenya

Lesotho

Mozambique

Oman

Saudi Arabia

Sri Lanka

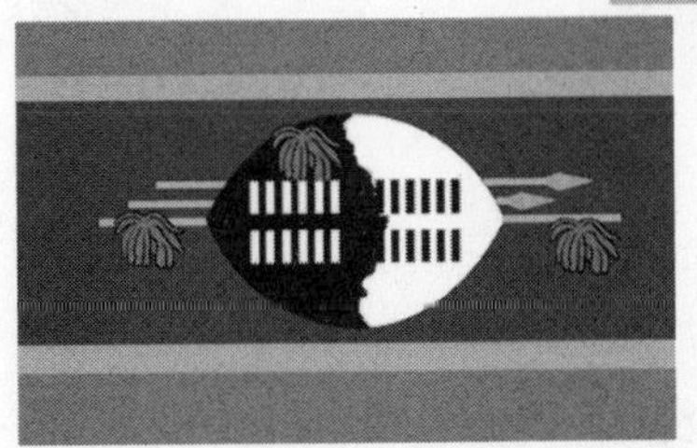

Swaziland

THE TEN YEARS' WAR

The longest of three wars fought for the independence of Cuba from Spain commenced on 10 October 1868 and almost ended within days when the patriotic army of Carlos Manuel de Céspedes, a wealthy plantation owner, failed to capture its first target, the town of Yara. The revolutionary urge, nonetheless, proved contagious, and guerilla movements sprang up in the east of the island that lent support. De Céspedes chose to act as though Cuba had already slipped the Spanish yoke, convening on 10 April 1869 a constitutional assembly in Guáimaro, where he was elected president. His unruly reign was later ended by the assembly, and he would be killed in an ambush on 27 February 1874, but guerilla activities in the regions of Camagüey and Oriente were sufficiently successful for the Spanish to retaliate with an unpopular harshness. In the negotiations of the Peace of Zanjon that ended conflict in February 1878, Spain agreed to end slavery. Not quite twenty years later, when the USS *Maine* exploded in Havana harbour, the US sent troops and sank the Spanish fleet off Santiago de Cuba; Spain formally turned over government to the US from 1 January 1899, and an elected local administration took control on 20 May 1902—the anniversary is still commemorated as Día de la República (Republic Day).

TEN SONGS WITH 'TEN' IN THE TITLE

'Count to Ten'. . . . . The Clean (1986)
'DC-10' . . . . Audio Adrenaline (1994)
'8x10'. . . . . Bill Anderson (1964)
'Force 10'. . . . . Rush (1987)
'Hang 10'. . . . . The Ramones (1976)
'News at 10'. . . . . The Vapors (1980)
'Song 10'. . . . . Zebrahead (1998)
'Ten-Bone' . . . . Benny Goodman (1959)
'Ten Days' . . . . Celine Dion (2002)
'Top 10' . . . . Gregory Isaacs (1984)

Christmas Feasts

The following six feasts are celebrated during the Festive Season: Christmas Day (25 December), St Stephen's Day (26 December), St John the Evangelist's Day (27 December), Holy Innocents' Day (28 December), Circumcision (1 January), Epiphany (6 January).

Dog Days

The hottest time of the year in the northern hemisphere, when dogs were, according to Pliny the Elder, 'most ready to run mad'. Dated, in some accounts, from the cosmical rising of Sirius (Canis Major) on 3 July, and extending forty days.

Egyptian Days

In the Christian religion from the fourth to the seventeenth centuries, days considered inauspicious for all activities, especially bloodletting. With some variations, they were as follows: 1 and 25 January; 4 and 26 February, 1 and 28 March, 10 and 20 April, 3 and 25 May, 10 and 16 June, 13 and 22 July, 1 and 30 August, 3 and 21 September, 3 and 22 October, 5 and 28 November, 7 and 22 December.

Ides

In the Roman calendar, the fifteenth day in each thirty-one-day month, the thirteenth in others. From the Etruscan word meaning 'divide'. In Latin, the *Eidus* or *Idus*.

Kalends

In the Roman calendar, the first day of each month. From the archaic verb *kalare* 'to proclaim'. In Latin, the *Kalendae*.

Quarter Days

When rents, interests and other charges are to be paid quarterly, English custom is for them to be settled on the four Quarter Days: Lady Day (25 March), Midsummer Day (24 June), Michaelmas (29 September) and Christmas (25 December).

Red Letter Days

In Great Britain, the days of ecclestiastical and civil significance on which judges of the Queen's Bench wear scarlet robes: Conversion of St Paul (25 January), Purification (2 February), Accession of HM the Queen (6 February), Ash Wednesday, St David's Day (1 March), Annunciation (25 March), Birthday of HM the Queen (21 April), St Mark (25 April), St Philip and St James (1 May), St Matthias (14 May), Ascension, Coronation of HM the Queen (2 June), Birth of HRH the Duke of Edinburgh (10 June), St Barnabas (11 June), Official Queen's Birthday, St John the Baptist (24 June), St Peter (29 June), St Thomas (3 July), St James (25 July), St Luke (18 October), St Simon and St Jude (28 October), All Saints' Day (1 November), Lord Mayor's Day (second Saturday in November), Birthday of HRH the Prince of Wales (14 November), St Andrew's Day (30 November).

Rogation Days

Christian appropriation of a Roman custom, the *Robigalia*, when farmers proceeded through their cornfields praying for relief from *robigo* (mildew). They became fasting days on which intercessory prayers were offered, rogation coming from the Latin *rogare,* to ask. Rogation Sunday is the fifth Sunday after Easter; the following Monday, Tuesday and Wednesday are the Minor Rogations.

Tenebrae

The last three days of Holy Week, the week preceeding Easter Sunday: Maundy Thursday, Good Friday and Holy Saturday, so called from the Latin for 'darkness' because of the custom at services for extinguishing candles, one by one, as each Psalm ended.

Term Days

The Scottish equivalent of Quarter Days, fixed by Acts of 1690 and 1693, are the four Term Days: Candlemas (2 February), Whitsunday (15 May), Lammas (1 August) and Martinmas (11 November).

TEN CRICKETERS' DEATHS

Abdul Aziz, Karachi (1942–1959)
Struck over the heart by an off-break.

Harry Bagshaw, umpire (1859–1927)
Buried in his umpire's coat with a cricket ball in his hand.

Frank Bryant, West Australian cricket official (1908–1984)
Died watching Sheffield Shield final, which his state later won.

Thomas Burge, Queensland cricket official (1903–1957)
Died while listening to his son Peter batting on radio.

Andy Ducat, Surrey (1886–1942)
A heart attack while representing his Home Guard unit against another at Lord's; he was 29 not out at the time.

Donald Eligon (1910–1937)
From blood poisoning caused by a nail in his cricket boot.

Aubrey Faulkner, Transvaal, South Africa (1881–1930)
Gassed himself at his Walham Green indoor cricket school, leaving the note: 'I am off to another sphere via the small bat-drying room. Better call in a policeman to do the investigating.'

Charles Grace, last surviving son of Dr W. G. Grace (1882–1938)
Died while playing a match at Hawkhurst.

Arthur H. Gregory, New South Wales (1861–1929)
From blood poisoning, after falling from a tram on the way home from the funeral of nephew, Test captain Syd.

George Porter, umpire (1861–1908)
Died of complications from sunstroke.

Alfred Shaw, Nottinghamshire, England (1842–1907)
Proposed that he be buried twenty-two yards from his comrade Arthur Shrewsbury, so that he might 'send him down a ball occasionally'.

TEN ABUSIVE EXPRESSIONS INCORPORATING THE WORD 'HEAD'

BLOCKHEAD	'No man but a blockhead ever wrote, except for money.'	Dr Johnson in Boswell's *Life of Samuel Johnson* (1791)
BONEHEAD	'James was a bonehead. I give you that.'	Arthur Conan Doyle, *His Last Bow* (1917)
CABBAGEHEAD	'Thou foul and filthy cabbagehead.'	Aphra Behn, *False Count* (1682)
CHEESEHEAD	'You let this cheesehead insult me?'	Raymond Chandler, *The Big Sleep* (1939)
DUNDERHEAD	'Shall I be called as many blockheads, numskulls, doddypooles, dunderheads—and other unsavoury appellations.'	Laurence Sterne, *Tristram Shandy* (1767)
FATHEAD	'If you want any further proof of your young man's fat-headedness, mark that.'	P. G. Wodehouse, *Something Fresh* (1915)
FLATHEAD	'Greenhorns, flatheads!'	Mark Twain, *Huckleberry Finn* (1884)
LOGGERHEAD:	'Ah, you whoreson loggerhead!'	William Shakespeare, *Love's Labour's Lost* (1595)
MEATHEAD	'Honeybunch! Listen to the meathead!'	H. I. Phillips, *Private Purkey's Private Peace* (1945)
PINHEAD	'There's just as many pinheads on State Street as you'll find out in the woods.'	George Ade, *Artie* (1896)

THE TEN GREAT MASTERS OF SIKHISM

First	Guru Nanak Dev	(1469–1539)
Second	Guru Angad Dev	(1504–1552)
Third	Guru Amar Das	(1479–1574)
Fourth	Guru Ram Das	(1534–1581)
Fifth	Guru Arjan Dev	(1563–1606)
Sixth	Guru Hargobind	(1595–1644)
Seventh	Guru Har Rai	(1630–1661)
Eighth	Guru Harkrishan	(1656–1664)
Ninth	Guru Tegh Bahadur	(1621–1675)
Tenth	Guru Gobind Singh	(1666–1708)

TEN BLACK DAYS

Black Monday 15 October 1945
So called by plantation owners in Papua New Guinea, the day when the Australian government cancelled all native labour contracts.

Black Monday 19 October 1987
On the New York Stock Exchange, the Dow Jones Industrial average fell 22.6 per cent, its largest one-day decline.

Black Tuesday 12 November 1912
The darkest day in New Zealand labour history, when a six-month strike by goldminers in Waihi was broken by the storming of the miners' hall by strike-breakers and police, and leader Fred Evans was beaten to death.

Black Wednesday 9 January 1878
The summary mass sacking of 300 Victorian civil servants, including leading department officials, judges, coroners and magistrates, by the

Berry government from the Legislative Assembly, in the face of the Legislative Council's blocking of supply.

Black Wednesday 16 September 1992
The grimmest day in the history of the Bank of England when, after spending £4 billion to defend it against speculators, it had to recommend sterling's withdrawal from the European Exchange Rate Mechanism.

Black Thursday 24 October 1929
The first sign that the 1920s stockmarket boom was ending, a wave of panic selling abating only when New York Stock Exchange boss Richard Whitney intervened. When the plunge resumed on Monday and Tuesday, however, nothing could stem it.

Black Friday 13 January 1939
The culmination of a week of unstoppable bushfires throughout Victoria: seventy-one died, 1000 were injured, 3000 left homeless and more than 30,000 affected.

Black Friday 24 September 1869
A brief but dramatic Wall Street crisis caused by the actions of James J. Fisk and Jay Gould, two notorious speculators, in their attempt to corner the US gold market.

Black Saturday 18 January 2003
Applied to bushfires that swept through residential suburbs of Canberra, killing four people and destroying 530 homes. It had earlier been associated with bushfires that swept New South Wales on 10 December 1938.

Black Sunday 6 February 1938
A surf calamity at Bondi Beach in which a backwash from shore and three huge waves in quick succession swept about 300 bathers hundreds of metres out to sea. Seventy lifeguards swam to the rescue, but five bathers died.

Both before and after the completion of his Ninth Symphony in Vienna in 1824, Ludwig van Beethoven (1770–1827) sketched numerous passages of the first movement of what he intended to be his Tenth Symphony, the last of which dates from October 1825. He was bedridden from December 1826 with cirrhosis of the liver, raging when he was visited: 'Here I have been lying for four months. One must at last lose patience!' Even then, however, he was intent on completing the work, out of gratitude to the Philharmonic Society of London, who had sent £100 to ease his suffering: 'I will compose a grand overture for them, and a symphony.'

How much survives of the Tenth Symphony has been a matter a conjecture among musicologists since. Beethoven's friend Karl Holz (1798–1858) claimed to have heard him play the first movement on a piano, describing an introduction in E-flat major and an allegro in C minor. The violinist Anton Schindler (1795–1864), Beethoven's first biographer, also hinted that the work was well advanced, leading to speculation that an intact draft survives. The sketches, which mention parts for horns, strings, timpani and woodwind, have been pored over by, among others, the French composer Erik Satie, who thought them 'fully proportioned, rich in ideas, with exact developments'.

The most elaborate archaeological efforts have been undertaken by Dr Barry Cooper (b. 1949), author of *Beethoven and the Creative Process* (1993), a study of Beethoven's working methods, who created a version of the first movement by assembling the 250 bars of sketches that survive in various workbooks, adding harmonies and linking passages, then orchestrating it in Beethovenesque style: he believes that the result, which he has recorded, is 'not exactly what Beethoven would have written' but 'far closer to Beethoven's Tenth Symphony than anything previously heard'. It was first recorded by the London Symphony Orchestra conducted by Wyn Morris in 1988, and by the Birmingham Symphony Orchestra conducted by Walter Weller four years later.

THE TEN SEFIROT

The Ten Sefirot of the Jewish Kabbala, from which the soul derives its ten corresponding soul powers, and which form the heart to all Kabbalistic theology and theosophy, are as follows:

> INTELLECT: *Chochma* (spontaneous creativity), *Bina* (understanding), *Daat* (knowledge).
>
> SOUL: *Chesed* (love, kindness), *Gevura* (fortitude, restrictive power), *Tiferet* (compassion), *Netzach* (perseverance), *Hod* (surrender, acknowledgment), *Yesod* (combining of aforesaid qualities), *Malchut* (receiving upon oneself the yoke of God's sovereignty).

TEN COMPUTER COMMANDMENTS

Proposed by the Computer Ethics Institute, a project of the Brookings Institution, a Washington think tank:

1. Thou shalt not use a computer to harm other people.
2. Thou shalt not interfere with other people's computer work.
3. Thou shalt not snoop around in other people's computer files.
4. Thou shalt not use a computer to steal.
5. Thou shalt not use a computer to bear false witness.
6. Thou shalt not copy or use proprietary software for which you have not paid.
7. Thou shalt not use other people's computer resources without authorisation or proper compensation.
8. Thou shalt not appropriate other people's intellectual output.
9. Thou shalt think about the social consequences of the program you are writing or the system you are designing.
10. Thou shalt always use a computer in ways that ensure consideration and respect for your fellow humans.

TEN FICTIONAL MICE

NAME	AUTHOR	TITLE
Anatole	Eve Titus	*Anatole* (1956)
Lives in 'small mouse village' near Paris; affects smock and beret.		
Miss Bianca	Margery Sharp	*The Rescuers* (1959)
Chairwoman of rodent NGO, Mouse Prisoners' Aid Society.		
Peter Churchmouse	Margot Austin	*Peter Churchmouse* (1941)
Shares Parson Pease-Porridge's church with Gabriel Churchkitten and Trumpet Churchdog.		
Mrs Frisby	Robert O'Brien	*Mrs Frisby and the Rats of Nimh* (1959)
Sole provider fieldmouse befriended by genius rats.		
Stuart Little	E. B. White	*Stuart Little* (1945)
Mouse child of human parents.		
Manxmouse	Paul Gallico	*Manxmouse* (1968)
Ceramic freak animated by clock striking thirteen; destined to confront nemesis Manx Cat.		
Mary Mouse	Enid Blyton	*Mary Mouse and the Doll's House* (1942)
Afflicted with wearisome cleaning fetish; marries into doll family.		
Ralph	Beverley Cleary	*The Mouse and the Motorcycle* (1965)
Lives behind skirting board of room 215 of Mountain View Inn; rides miniature motorbike.		
Reepicheep	C. S. Lewis	*The Chronicles of Narnia* (1939–56)
Prince Caspian's chivalrous, garrulous ally; features in three of the seven novels.		
Mrs Tittlemouse	Beatrix Potter	*The Tale of Mrs Tittlemouse* (1910)
Fastidious woodmouse dealing with incorrigibly messy toad lodger, Mr Jackson.		

Swiss adventurer Johann Ludwig Burckhardt (1784–1817) first visited Africa aged twenty-two, becoming so fluent in the local dialects and customs that he was able to pass as an Arab merchant and become one of the first Westerners to visit Mecca, then forbidden to non-Muslims. *Arabic Proverbs*, his posthumously published translation of a hundred-year-old compilation by Sheref ed dyn Ibn Asad annotated to 'interest and gratify the Orientalist', contains a host of sayings familiar in sentiment also to the occidentalist.

اذا كترت النواتية غرقت الركب

If the sailors become too numerous, the ship sinks.
(*Too many cooks spoil the broth.*)

العب مع العبد يوريک شِقه

Play with a slave, he will show to thee his hinder parts.
(*Familiarity breeds contempt.*)

تكون نار تصبح رماد

It may be a fire; on the morrow it will be ashes.
(*Violent passions easily subside.*)

حبيبک من تحبه و لو كان قرد

Thy beloved is the object that thou lovest, were it even a monkey.
(*Love is blind.*)

زامر الحي ما يطّرب

The fifer of his [own] camp does not rejoice.
(*A prophet is not without honour, except in his own country.*)

عين لا تري قلب لا يحزن

[When] the eye does not see, the heart does not grieve.
(*See no evil, feel no evil.*)

قد يتوقّي السيف و هو مغمّد

Truly, the sword inspires dread even in its scabbard.
(*Walk softly, and carry a big stick.*)

لو لا الكسورة ما كانت الفاخورة

Were it not for fractures, there would be no pottery.
(*Every cloud has a silver lining.*)

وصل السكين للعظم

The knife has reached the bone.
(*Cut to the quick.*)

الف كرّكي في اجوّ ما تعوّض عصفور في الكفّ

A thousand cranes in the air are not worth one sparrow in the fist.
(*A bird in the hand is worth two in the bush.*)

G10

Intended as a forum for co-ordination of credit policy between central bankers, the G10 was established in 1962 and headquartered in Paris. Despite its name, it currently consists of eleven nations: the United States of America, Canada, Italy, Germany, France, the United Kingdom, Japan, the Netherlands, Belgium, Sweden and Switzerland. Its most recent meeting was in Basel in January 2004.

TEN FAMOUS CODED MESSAGES

1. NIITAKA-YAMA-MOBERE

Japanese for 'Climb Mount Nitaka'. Signal to Chuichi Nagumo's aircraft carrier fleet from commander-in-chief Isoruku Yamamoto to initiate the attack on Pearl Harbor, 7 December 1941.

2. BRADMAN WILL BE BATTING TOMORROW

Signal to Allied troops, warning them of the impending artillery bombardment of the Monte Cassino monastery, 14 March 1944.

3. THE FIRST FOUR NOTES OF BEETHOVEN'S FIFTH SYMPHONY

Broadcast by radio from London, these notes, which also happen to form the letter V (for Victory) in Morse Code, alerted members of the French resistance to the landings at Normandy on D-Day, 6 June 1944.

4. ONE IF BY LAND, TWO IF BY SEA

A code agreed on 11 April 1775 between Paul Revere (1734–1818) and the 'Sons of Liberty' committee of Charlestown to indicate the nature of British attack in case he himself was prevented from leaving Boston to pass on the news: one lantern in the bell tower of Boston's Christ Church would indicate a march 'by land' out Boston Neck; two would indicate rowing 'by sea' across the Charles River to Cambridge. Two were shown a week later when Revere was sent for by Dr Joseph Warren and instructed to make his famous ride to Lexington, Massachusetts, to warn Samuel Adams and John Hancock that British troops were marching to arrest them. The origination of the code is commemorated in Henry Longfellow's famous poem 'Paul Revere's Ride':

He said to his friend, 'If the British march
By land or sea from the town to-night,
Hang a lantern aloft in the belfry arch
Of the North Church tower, as a signal light, —
One, if by land, and two, if by sea;
And I on the opposite shore will be...

5. SMAISMRMILMEPOETALEUMIBUNENUGTTAUIRAS

In 1610, Galileo Galilei used this anagram to communicate his discovery that two moons orbited Mars (which would later be named Phobos and Deimos). Johannes Kepler managed to disentangle the anagram to make the Latin greeting *Salve umbisteneum geminatum Martia proles* ('Hail, twin companionship, children of Mars') which confirmed a prediction he had made to the same effect.

6. PLEASE INFORM COCKCROFT AND MAUD RAY, KENT

A postscript to a wire sent by physicist Niels Bohr to friends and colleagues in Britain shortly after the German occupation of Denmark during World War II informing them of his safety. It actually enjoined them to 'make uranium day and night'.

7.

mm.rnlls	*esrevel*	*seecIde*
sgtssmf	*vnteief*	*niedrke*
kt,samn	*atrateS*	*saodrrn*
emtnaeI	*nvaect*	*rrilSa*
Atsaar	*nvcrc*	*ieaabs*
ccrmi	*eevtVl*	*frAntv*
dt,iac	*oseibo*	*KediiI*

This reversed runic cipher left by the sixteenth-century alchemist Arne Saknussemm is thus unravelled by the adventurers in Jules Verne's *Journey to the Centre of the Earth* (1874):

In Sneffels Joculis craterem quem delibat
Umbra Scartaris Julii intra calendas descende,
Audax viator, et terrestre centrum attinges.
Quod feci, Arne Saknussemm.

Which, translated from the Latin, reveals the thrilling intelligence: 'Descend, bold traveller, into the crater of the jokul [volcano] of Sneffels, which the shadow of Scartaris touches before the kalends of July, and you will attain the centre of the earth; which I have done, Arne Saknussemm.'

8. A BOY IS BORN! A BOY IS BORN!

Message to government colleagues sent by Indian prime minister Indira Gandhi announcing the successful conclusion of the Simla Accord on 2 July 1972 with Pakistan's Zulfikar Ali Bhutto, committing their nations to respect a ceasefire line called the Line of Control. Failure of the negotiations would have precipitated the code: 'A girl is born! A girl is born!'

9. TUBE ALLOYS

Perhaps the most famous coded expression of all, standing in for the atomic bomb while the Manhattan Project was in progress. It was assigned during a meeting between Winston Churchill and Franklin Roosevelt about the terms of the bomb's use at The Citadel in Quebec in August 1943, heading a document entitled 'Articles of Agreement Governing Collaboration between the Authorities of the USA and the UK in the Matter of Tube Alloys'.

10.

130 13042 13401 8501 115 3528 416 17214 6491 11310 18147 18222 21560 10247 11518 23677 13605 3494 14936 98092 5905 11311 10392 10371 0302 21290 5151 39695 23571 17504 11269 18276 18101 0317 0228 17694 4473 23284 22200 19452 21589 67893 5569 13918 8958 12137 1333 4725 4458 5905 17166 13851 4458 17149 14471 6706 13850 12224 6929 14991 7382 1585767893 14218 36477 5870 17553 67893 5870 5454 16102 15217 22801 17138 21001 17388 7446 23638 18222 6719 14331 15021 23845 3158 23552 22096 21604 4797 9497 22464 20855 4377 23610 18140 22260 5905 13347 20420 39689 13732 20667 6929 5275 18507 52262 1340 22049 13339 11265 22295 10439 14814 4178 6992 8784 7632 7357 6926 52262 11267 21100 21272 9346 9559 22464 15874 18502 18500 15857 2188 5376 7381 98092 16127 13486 9350 9220 76036 14219 5144 2831 17920 11347 17142 11264 7667 7762 15099 9110 10482 97556 3569 3670

On 16 January 1917, German foreign secretary Arthur Zimmermann dispatched a telegram to Count von Bernstorff, his ambassador in Washington, who was to forward it to the Imperial German minister in Mexico, von Eckhardt. It proposed an alliance between Germany and Mexico for a joint war against the United States. Intercepted by Room 40, a secret unit of British Naval Intelligence in Whitehall, the message was decoded by two cryptographers: Nigel de Gray, a young publisher from William Heinemann, and William Montgomery, a clergyman.

On the first of February we intend to begin unrestricted submarine warfare. In spite of this, it is our endeavour to keep the United States of America neutral.

If this attempt is not successful, we propose an alliance on the following basis with Mexico: that we shall make war together and together make peace. We shall give general financial support, and it is understood that Mexico is to reconquer the lost territory in New Mexico, Texas and Arizona. The details are left to you for settlement.

You are instructed to inform the President of Mexico of the above in the greatest confidence as soon as it is certain that there will be an outbreak of war with the United States and suggest that the President of Mexico, on his own initiative, should communicate with Japan suggesting adherence at once to this plan; at the same time, offer to mediate between Germany and Japan.

Please call to the attention of the President of Mexico that the employment of ruthless submarine warfare now promises to compel England to make peace in a few months.

Where the loss of American lives in the sinking of the *Lusitania* on 7 May 1915 had been insufficient on its own as a *casus belli*, the so-called 'Zimmermann Telegram' finally convinced a thunderstruck American president Woodrow Wilson that his country should make common cause with the Allies. The story is supremely well told in Barbara Tuchman's *The Zimmermann Telegram* (1959).

TEN IRISH HUNGER-STRIKERS

On 1 March 1981, Irish republicans incarcerated in Maze Prison began a series of hunger strikes to protest against the rescission five years earlier of their status as political prisoners. The members of the Irish Republican Army and Irish National Liberation Army sought the British government's acquiescence to five demands:

1. The Right not to wear a prison uniform.
2. The Right not to do prison work.
3. The Right of free association with other prisoners.
4. The Right to organise their own educational and recreational facilities.
5. The Right to one visit, one letter and one parcel per week.

Within eight months, ten had died. Their names, organisations, date of death and length of strike were as follows:

Bobby Sands	IRA	5 May 1981	66 days
Francis Hughes	IRA	12 May 1981	59 days
Patsy O'Hara	INLA	21 May 1981	61 days
Raymond McCreesh	IRA	21 May 1981	61 days
Joe McDonnell	IRA	8 July 1981	61 days
Martin Hurson	IRA	13 July 1981	46 days
Kevin Lynch	INLA	1 August 1981	71 days
Kieran Doherty	IRA	2 August 1981	73 days
Thomas McElwee	IRA	8 August 1981	62 days
Michael Devine	INLA	20 August 1981	60 days

TEN A SERIES PAPER SIZES

A1 841 x 594mm	A2 594 x 420mm
A3 420 x 297mm	A4 297 x 210mm
A5 210 x 148mm	A6 148 x 105mm
A7 105 x 74mm	A8 74 x 52mm
A9 52 x 37mm	A10 37 x 26mm

David Jones (1895–1974)
British poet/painter, notable for his epic poem of World War I *In Parenthesis*: 'You can hear the silence of it: / you can hear the rat of no-man's-land / rut out intricacies, / weasel-out his patient workings / scrut, scrut, scrut, / harrow-out earthly, trowel his cunning paw.'

Inigo Jones (1573–1652)
British architect. Designer *inter alia* of the Queen's House, Greenwich, the Banqueting House, Whitehall. Espoused the view that architecture 'should be solid, proportional according to the rules, masculine and unaffected'.

Rev. Jim Jones (1931–1978)
American cult leader, the People's Temple, who presided over the mass death of its 914 members at their Jonestown commune in Guyana on 18 November 1978. 'We are not committing suicide,' he stated. 'It's a revolutionary act.'

John Paul Jones (1747–1792)
American admiral. Famous for his engagement with HMS *Serapis* off Farnborough Head on 23 September 1779, where he was asked if he would surrender his blazing ship *Bonhomme Richard* and replied: 'I have not yet begun to fight.'

Everett LeRoi Jones (b. 1934)
American dramatist aka Imamu Amiri Baraka. Best known for his play *Midstream* (1963): 'God has been replaced, as he has all over the West, with respectability and air conditioning.'

Mary Harris 'Mother' Jones (1830–1930)
American labour activist, a founder of the Industrial Workers of the World. Her motto, cited in *The Autobiography of Mother Jones* (1925): 'Pray for the dead and fight like hell for the living.'

Bobby Jones (1902–1971)
American golfer. Winner of four US Opens and thirteen British

Opens. Of the degenerative syringomyelia with which he was diagnosed in 1948 and which steadily crippled him, he responded stoically: 'We all have to play the ball as it lies.'

Steve Jones (b. 1955)
British guitarist, Sex Pistols. Responsible for their ban from television on 1 December 1976 when he referred to Thames TV's Bill Grundy as a 'fucking rotter'.

William Jones (1746–1794)
British jurist and liberal noted for scepticism and irreverence: 'My opinion is that power should always be distrusted in whatever hands it is placed.'

Vinny Jones (b. 1965)
Hatchet-faced British footballer turned actor. Formerly a hod carrier. Philosophy: 'Winning doesn't really matter as long as you win.'

EUGENE O'NEILL'S TEN LOST PLAYS

During the wanderings of his early life when he was among other things a gold prospector, an actor and a newspaper reporter, and before his Pulitzer Prize-winning *Beyond the Horizon* (1920), Eugene O'Neill (1888–1953) wrote a host of short dramas, some of them performed by the Provincetown Players. Ten of them became known as his 'lost' plays, and were not published until 1964:

A Wife for a Life
The Web
Fog
Abortion
Servitude
Thirst
Warnings
Recklessness
The Movie Man
The Sniper

Exodus 20:1–17, King James Version:

1. And God spake all these words, saying,
2. I am the LORD thy God, which have brought thee out of the land of Egypt, out of the house of bondage.
3. **Thou shalt have no other gods before me.**
4. **Thou shalt not make unto thee any graven image**, or any likeness of any thing that is in heaven above, or that is in the earth beneath, or that is in the water under the earth:
5. Thou shalt not bow down thyself to them, nor serve them: for I the LORD thy God am a jealous God, visiting the iniquity of the fathers upon the children unto the third and fourth generation of them that hate me;
6. And shewing mercy unto thousands of them that love me, and keep my commandments.
7. **Thou shalt not take the name of the LORD thy God in vain**; for the LORD will not hold him guiltless that taketh his name in vain.
8. **Remember the sabbath day**, to keep it holy.
9. Six days shalt thou labour, and do all thy work.
10. But the seventh day is the sabbath of the LORD thy God: in it thou shalt not do any work, thou, nor thy son, nor thy daughter, thy manservant, nor thy maidservant, nor thy cattle, nor thy stranger that is within thy gates:
11. For in six days the LORD made heaven and earth, the sea, and all that in them is, and rested the seventh day: wherefore the LORD blessed the sabbath day, and hallowed it.
12. **Honour thy father and thy mother**: that thy days may be long upon the land which the LORD thy God giveth thee.
13. **Thou shalt not kill.**
14. **Thou shalt not commit adultery.**

15. **Thou shalt not steal.**
16. **Thou shalt not bear false witness against thy neighbour.**
17. **Thou shalt not covet thy neighbour's house,** thou shalt not covet thy neighbour's wife, nor his manservant, nor his maidservant, nor his ox, nor his ass, nor any thing that is thy neighbour's.

TEN GOLFING COLLOQUIALISMS

CHILLI-DIPPING: Taking a chunk from the fairway in the act of playing a shot. Also known as 'more shit than hit'.

DRIVE FOR SHOW, PUTT FOR DOUGH: Aphorism suggesting that the short game is what distinguishes good players from bad.

GOING IN ON THE FLY: An approach shot that lands in the hole without stopping on the green.

GRIP IT AND RIP IT: The injunction to hit drives long with the maximum backswing.

ON THE APRON: A ball sitting on the grass just in front of the green.

PLAYING A STABLEFORD: A variant on the game involving the award of points rather than the counting of strokes.

TAKING A MULLIGAN: Enjoying a second go if one fails to tee off successfully on the first hole.

TAKING THE HAZARD OUT OF PLAY: When confronted by a hazard, using a club with a limited range to ensure that one's shot falls short.

THROUGH THE BACK DOOR: A putt that falls late having appeared to pass the hole.

USING THE BORROW: Playing a shot that takes account of the slope of the green.

TEN MUSES

The nine true muses of classical antiquity are: Calliope (Epic Poetry), Clio (History), Erato (Love Poetry), Euterpe (Music), Melpomene (Tragedy), Polyhymnia (Sacred Poetry), Terpsichore (Dancing), Thalia (Comedy), Urania (Astronomy). In his *Anthologia Palantia*, Plato proposed as a tenth muse the poet Sappho of Lesbos: 'Some say the muses are nine—how careless—behold, Sappho of Lesbos is the tenth.' It was a title subsequently conferred on a string of literary women, including Antoinette Duligier dela Garde Deshoulieres (1638–1694), Madeleine de Scudery (1607–1701), Queen Christina of Sweden (1626–1689) and Hannah More (1745–1833).

FOOTBALL'S TEN GOLDEN RULES

Len Smith, coach of Fitzroy and Richmond in the 1950s and 1960s and older brother of the more famous Norm, was one of the foremost seers in the history of Australian rules. A solid backman during a 93-game career cut short by military service, he believed in simple, commonsense principles, which he once distilled as 'The Golden Rules'.

1. Get the ball through the goals in the quickest manner possible but remember that kicking the ball into an opponent is a football sin (attacks should be started from the half-back line, and the quickest route to goal employed).
2. Two men together at all times.
3. No packs or crushes.
4. Crumbs, crumbs, crumbs (remember that three out of four possessions are gained by the ball spilling from a pack).
5. Play close to opponent (backmen).
6. Team spirit, intelligent talking (call specific instructions to your teammates).
7. Mind your opponent.
8. Stand on the mark.
9. Stop your opponent from playing on.
10. Tackle opponents in possession of the ball.

TEN HEADLINES FROM LONDON'S SUN

Between April 1981 and January 1994, Kelvin MacKenzie (b. 1946) was editor of the *Sun*, perfecting a house style that made it what the *Economist* described as 'the rottweiler of British journalism'. Known to his staff as 'MacFrenzie', and to *Private Eye* as 'Gobshite', his motto was 'Shock and Amaze on Every Page', but his particular joy was the screaming front-page headline, some so resonant that they have defied the definition of news as anything less interesting tomorrow than today.

STICK IT UP YOUR JUNTA
When Argentina offered a negotiated settlement to the Falkland Islands dispute.

GOTCHA!
After the sinking of the *General Belgrano* at the cost of 368 lives, April 1982.

KINNOCK'S PARTY OF PLONKERS
Welcoming Neil Kinnock as Labour leader, October 1983.

ZEE FRENCH ARE FEEL-THY: OFFICIAL
After a survey revealed that per capita soap use is lower in France than elsewhere in Europe.

FREDDIE STARR ATE MY HAMSTER
After the 'zany comic' put a hamster between two slices of bread and affected to eat it, March 1986.

PULPIT POOFS CAN STAY
After an Anglican synod discussion of homosexuality in the clergy.

BAA-BAA BAN ON SAD LITTLE DAN
After a child was forbidden from reciting 'Baa-Baa Black Sheep' on grounds it was racist.

SPECIAL NIGHTMARE ISSUE
Three days before the 1987 election, a medium polled the ranks of the dead about their voting intentions: Stalin was for Neil Kinnock, Churchill, Nelson and Boadicea for Margaret Thatcher.

UP YOURS, DELORS!
Against European integration, November 1990.

WILL THE LAST PERSON TO LEAVE BRITAIN PLEASE TURN OUT THE LIGHTS?
On the eve of the 1992 election, which Labour looked like winning.

TEN WAYS OF SERVING EGGS

Boiled
Scrambled
Coddled
Omelette
Oeuf a la neige
Fried
Poached
Hard-boiled
Shirred (aka baked eggs)
Soufflé

'It's very easy to talk,' said Mrs Mantalini. 'Not so easy to talk when one is eating a demnition egg,' replied Mr Mantalini; 'for the yolk runs down the waistcoat, and yolk of egg does not match any waistcoat but a yellow waistcoat, demmit.'

Nicholas Nickelby (1839) by Charles Dickens

THE TEN TEST CRICKET NATIONS

Australia (1877) — Bangladesh (2000) — England (1877) — India (1932) — New Zealand (1930) — Pakistan (1952) — South Africa (1889) — Sri Lanka (1982) — West Indies (1928) — Zimbabwe (1992)

WORLD'S TEN BUSIEST PORTS

The volumes handled by different ports, as calculated by the American Association of Port Authorities, are usually ranked one of two ways: by total volume measured in tonnes, or by container traffic measured in TEUs. TEU stands for 'Twenty-Foot Equivalent Unit'. Containers are normally counted in twenty-foot lengths. A twenty-foot container counts as one TEU, a forty-foot container as two TEUs, and so on.

Busiest Ports by Volume

1. Singapore
2. Rotterdam, Netherlands
3. South Louisiana, USA
4. Shanghai, China
5. Hong Kong, China
6. Houston, USA
7. Chiba, Japan
8. Nagoya, Japan
9. Ulsan, South Korea
10. Kwangyang, South Korea

Busiest Ports by Containers (TEUs)

1. Hong Kong, China
2. Singapore
3. Pusan, South Korea
4. Kaohsiung, Taiwan
5. Rotterdam, Netherlands
6. Shanghai, China
7. Los Angeles, USA
8. Long Beach, USA
9. Hamburg, Germany
10. Antwerp, Belgium

THE BIG TEN

Paramount body of American college athletics, more formally known as the Intercollegiate Conference of Faculty Representatives when it was founded in November 1895. For most of the twentieth century, it involved ten institutions: University of Illinois, University of Michigan, University of Minnesota, Northwestern University, Purdue University, University of Wisconsin, Indiana University, Ohio State University, State University of Iowa and Michigan State University (which joined after the withdrawal of University of Chicago). Since 1990, there has been an eleventh member: Pennsylvania State University.

TEN ATMOSPHERIC WEATHER MAP SYMBOLS

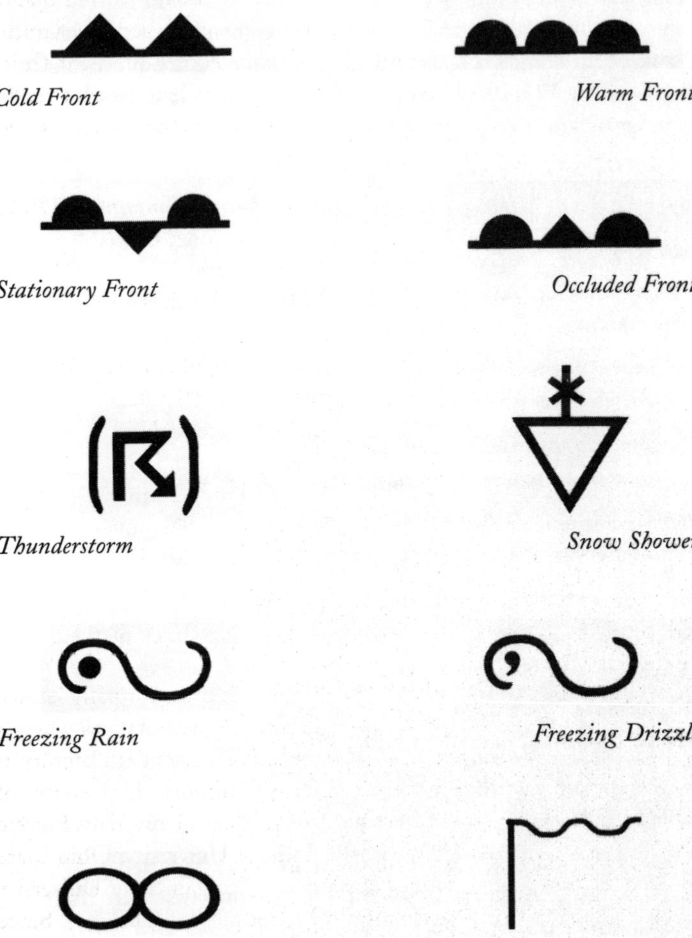

TEN YOGI-ISMS

'I didn't really say everything I said.'
This self-deprecation of Lawrence Peter 'Yogi' Berra (b. 1925) conveys also his other great gift. A decorated member of the New York Yankees for eighteen years and elected to the National Baseball Hall of Fame in 1972, Berra became just as famous for minting malapropisms, which came to be known as Yogi-isms.

'When you come to a fork in the road, take it.'

'That's his style of hitting. If you can't imitate him, don't copy him.'

'No, but he did a lot better than I thought he would.'
Asked whether New York Yankees' Don Mattingly had 'exceeded expectations'.

'If the guy was real poor, I'd give it back to him.'
Asked what he would do with $1 million.

'Yeah, what paper do you write for?'
Introduced to Ernest Hemingway and told he was a 'writer'.

'He must have done that one before he died.'
On seeing Steve McQueen in *The Magnificent Seven.*

'All these years, Jack, and you still can't spell my name.'
On receiving a cheque from KMOX Radio's Jack Buck marked 'Payable to Bearer'.

'Better make it four. I don't think I can eat eight.'
Asked how many slices he wanted his pizza cut.

'It gets late early out there.'
On the shadows at Yankee Stadium.

Told by Pittsburgh Private Phil Garner that he had used a Yogi-ism, Berra replied, 'What's a Yogi-ism?' He has since wised up. Berra is the author of two books of inspirational advice: *When You Come to a Fork in the Road, Take It* (2001) and *What Time Is It? Do You Mean Now?* (2002). A recent PBS documentary on his life was entitled *Déjà vu All over Again.*

10 RILLINGTON PLACE

A decrepit three-storey Victorian house abutting a factory wall at the end of a cul-de-sac of London's Notting Hill, whose ground floor was occupied from 1938 by John Reginald Halliday Christie, his wife Ethel nee Waddington, their dog and cat. Its address was made famous fifteen years later when Christie, a former postman, soldier and special constable, was revealed as one of the world's most compulsive and cold-blooded serial killers. Over a decade, the house was the scene of eight murders and became the location of eight ersatz graves:

August 1943 .... Ruth Fuerst, 21
October 1944 .... Muriel Eady, 31
November 1949.......................... Beryl Evans, 20
November 1949 .... Geraldine Evans, 1
December 1952.......................... Ethel Christie, 55
January 1953....................... Kathleen Maloney, 26
January 1953 .... Rita Nelson, 25
March 1953 .... Hectorina MacLennan, 26

Christie initially escaped suspicion. Timothy Evans, a lodger at Rillington Place, was convicted of the murder of his wife Beryl and infant daughter and hanged in March 1950. It was when Christie moved out in March 1953, and the house's new occupant discovered human remains, including the strangled corpse of Ethel Christie, that investigations resumed. Christie was arrested, convicted and hanged at Pentonville Prison, although he steadfastly declined to confess to killing Geraldine Evans; Timothy Evans' conviction was quashed in 1966.

Ludovic Kennedy's *10 Rillington Place* (1965) is one of the most popular books in the annals of true crime, although John Eddowes *The Two Killers of Rillington Place* (1994) has challenged supposition of Evans' innocence. For the sake of verisimilitude, Richard Fleischer's 1971 film adaptation of Kennedy's book starring Richard Attenborough was shot in another, near-identical house in Rillington Place. Soon after, the street was razed, and renamed Ruston Close—today Ruston Mews.

THE HOLLYWOOD TEN

A group of Hollywood screenwriters and directors who at the zenith of McCarthyism were accused of being members of the Communist Party and blacklisted. Subpoeanaed by the House Un-American Activities Committee (HUAC) in October 1947, they refused to answer questions about Communist influence in Hollywood labour unions. Six weeks later, the US House of Representatives voted 346-17 to approve citations for contempt of Congress. The day after, the leading Hollywood producers announced that unless they recanted they would be fired or suspended and not rehired. None did; they were sentenced to jail terms of between six months and a year in 1950. On release, the majority resumed work in the film industry under pseudonyms or behind 'fronts'. The Hollywood Ten and their major films were as follows:

Alvah Bessie . . . . *The Very Thought of You* (1944), *Objective Burma* (1945)
Herbert Biberman. . . . . *The Master Race* (1944), *Slaves* (1969)
Lester Cole . . . . *If I Had a Million* (1932), *Pursued* (1934)
Edward Dmytryk . . . . . . *Murder My Sweet* (1944)*, *Crossfire* (1947)
Ring Lardner Jnr . . . . *Woman of the Year* (1942), *MASH* (1970)
John Howard Lawson. . . . . . . *Blockade* (1938), *Counterattack* (1945)
Albert Maltz . . . . *Casablanca* (1942), *The Naked City* (1948)
Samuel Ornitz . . . . *They Live in Fear* (1944), *Circumstantial Evidence* (1945)
Adrian Scott . . . . *Keeping Company* (1940), *We Go Fast* (1941)
Dalton Trumbo . . . . *Exodus* (1960), *Spartacus* (1960)

* Adaptation of Raymond Chandler's *Farewell, My Lovely*

TEN JAPANESE AIRCRAFT CARRIERS FROM WORLD WAR II

Akagi — *Hiryu* — *Kaga* — *Ryujo* — *Shohu* — *Shokaku* — *Soryu* — *Taiho* — *Zuiho* — *Zuikaku*

TEN COMMON SYMBOLIC WASHING INSTRUCTIONS

Machine Wash, Normal

Machine Wash, Cold
30°C or 65–85°F

Machine Wash, Warm
40°C or 105°F

Machine Wash, Hot
50°C or 120°F

Machine Wash, Hot
60°C or 140°F

Machine Wash, Hot
70°C or 160°F

Machine Wash, Hot
95°C or 200°F

Machine Wash, Permanent Press

Machine Wash, Gentle or Delicate

Hand Wash

TEN OLDEST EUROPEAN BUSINESSES

Name	*Date*	*Industry*
Stora Kopparbergs Bergslags	c. 1000	Timber, metal products
Bayerische Statsbrauerei	1040	Brewery
Klosterbrauerei Scheyern	1119	Brewery
Mansfeld Aktiengesellschaft fur Bergbau und Huttenbetrieb	1200	Copper
Lowenapotheke	1241	Pharmacy
Clerget-Buffet et Fils	1270	Vintners
Raoul Clerget et Fils	1270	Vintners
Urquell Brewery	1295	Brewery
Burgspital zum Heilegen Geist	1319	Brewery
Moulin Papier Richard-de-Bas	1326	Papermakers

TEN REASONS FOR THE POPULARITY OF THE TOP TEN

In his delightful book *A Mathematician Reads the Newspaper* (1995), Professor John Allen Paulos advances ten reasons why the top ten has become such a staple of the modern media:

1. Ten is a common and familiar number, the base of our number system. Numbers are rounded to ten or to multiples of ten or tenths. The resulting distortion, of course, need not have much to do with reality. We're told, for example, that we use 10 per cent of our brain power, that 10 per cent of us consume 90 per cent of the world's resources, and that decades define us. (Is there anything more vapid than explanation by decade? In the free love, anti-war sixties, hippies felt so and so; the greed of the eighties led yuppies

to do such and such, sullen and unread Generation X-ers never do anything.)

2. People like information to be encapsulated; they're impatient with long, discursive explanations. They want the bare facts and they want them now.
3. The list is consistent with a linear approach to problems. Nothing is complex or convoluted; every factor can be ranked. If we do a, b, c, then x, y, or z will happen. Proportionality reigns.
4. It's a kind of ritual. Numbers are associated with rites, and this is a perfect example.
5. It has biblical resonances: the Ten Commandments being one of its first instances. Others are the ten plagues on the Egyptians, the ten days between Rosh Hashanah and Yom Kippur, the requirement that ten men be present for public prayer, and Joseph's ten brothers.
6. The list can be a complete story. It has a beginning: 1, 2, 3; a middle: 4, 5, 6, 7; and an end: 8, 9, 10. Many stories in the news are disconnected; the list is unitary.
7. It's easy to write; there is no need to come up with transitions. Or even complete sentences. The same holds for the 10, 50 and 100 YEARS AGO TODAY fillers.
8. It's flexible and capable of handling any subject. Since there are never any clear criteria for what constitutes an entry on such a list, items on short lists can easily be split, and those on long lists can just as easily be combined.
9. Lists are widely read (or heard) and talked about, but don't require much room in the paper or much airtime.
10. People realise it's an artificial form and like to see if it's going to run out of good points before it gets to ten.

INDEX